Don't
Let Anything
Dull Your
Sparkle

ALSO BY DOREEN VIRTUE

<u>Books/Calendars/Kits/Oracle Board</u>

21 Days to Higher Energy (with Robert Reeves, N.D.; available August 2017)

Father Therapy (with Andrew Karpenko; available November 2017)

How to Get Your Life Back (with Brigitte Parvin; available January 2018)

Fairy Foods (with Liana Werner-Gray; available April 2018)

10 Messages Your Angels Want You to Know

Veggie Momma (with Jenny Ross)

Awaken Your Indigo Power (with Charles Virtue)

The Courage to Be Creative

Nutrition for Intuition (with Robert Reeves, N.D.)

Angel Affirmations Calendar (for each individual year)

Earth Angel Realms

Living Pain-Free (with Robert Reeves, N.D.)

The Big Book of Angel Tarot (with Radleigh Valentine)

Angels of Abundance (with Grant Virtue)

Angel Dreams (with Melissa Virtue)

Angel Astrology 101 (with Yasmin Boland)

Angel Detox (with Robert Reeves, N.D.)

Assertiveness for Earth Angels

How to Heal a Grieving Heart (with James Van Praagh)

The Essential Doreen Virtue Collection

The Miracles of Archangel Gabriel

Mermaids 101

Flower Therapy (with Robert Reeves, N.D.)

Mary, Queen of Angels

Saved by an Angel

The Angel Therapy® Handbook

Angel Words (with Grant Virtue)

Archangels 101

The Healing Miracles of Archangel Raphael

The Art of Raw Living Food (with Jenny Ross)

Signs from Above (with Charles Virtue)

The Miracles of Archangel Michael

Angel Numbers 101

Solomon's Angels (a novel)

My Guardian Angel (with Amy Oscar)

Angel Blessings Candle Kit (with Grant Virtue; includes booklet, CD, journal, etc.)

Thank You, Angels! (children's book with Kristina Tracy)

Healing Words from the Angels

How to Hear Your Angels

Fairies 101

Daily Guidance from Your Angels

Divine Magic

How to Give an Angel Card Reading Kit

Angels 101

Angel Guidance Board

Crystal Therapy (with Judith Lukomski)

Connecting with Your Angels Kit (includes booklet, CD, journal, etc.)

The Crystal Children

Archangels & Ascended Masters

Earth Angels

Messages from Your Angels

Angel Visions II

Eating in the Light (with Becky Black, M.F.T., R.D.)

The Care and Feeding of Indigo Children

Angel Visions

Divine Prescriptions

Healing with the Angels

"I'd Change My Life If I Had More Time"

Divine Guidance

Chakra Clearing

Angel Therapy®

Constant Craving A–Z

Constant Craving

The Yo-Yo Diet Syndrome

Losing Your Pounds of Pain

Audio/CD Programs

The Healing Miracles of Archangel Raphael (unabridged audio book)

Angel Therapy® Meditations

Archangels 101 (abridged audio book)

Solomon's Angels (unabridged audio book)

Fairies 101 (abridged audio book)

Angel Medicine (available as both 1- and 2-CD sets)

Angels among Us (with Michael Toms)

Messages from Your Angels (abridged audio book)

Past-Life Regression with the Angels

Divine Prescriptions

The Romance Angels

Connecting with Your Angels

Manifesting with the Angels

Karma Releasing

Healing Your Appetite, Healing Your Life

Healing with the Angels

Divine Guidance

Chakra Clearing

DVD Program

How to Give an Angel Card Reading

Card Decks
(divination cards and guidebook)

Angels of Abundance Oracle Cards (with Radleigh Valentine; available July 2017)

Animal Tarot Cards (with Radleigh Valentine; available October 2017)

Butterfly Oracle Cards

Loving Words from Jesus

Fairy Tarot Cards (with Radleigh Valentine)

Archangel Gabriel Oracle Cards

Angel Answers Oracle Cards (with Radleigh Valentine)

Past Life Oracle Cards (with Brian Weiss, M.D.)

Guardian Angel Tarot Cards (with Radleigh Valentine)

Cherub Angel Cards for Children

Talking to Heaven Mediumship Cards (with James Van Praagh)

Archangel Power Tarot Cards (with Radleigh Valentine)

Flower Therapy Oracle Cards (with Robert Reeves)

Indigo Angel Oracle Cards (with Charles Virtue)

Angel Dreams Oracle Cards (with Melissa Virtue)

Mary, Queen of Angels Oracle Cards

Angel Tarot Cards (with Radleigh Valentine and Steve A. Roberts)

The Romance Angels Oracle Cards

Life Purpose Oracle Cards

Archangel Raphael Healing Oracle Cards

Archangel Michael Oracle Cards

Angel Therapy® Oracle Cards

Magical Messages from the Fairies Oracle Cards

Ascended Masters Oracle Cards

Daily Guidance from Your Angels Oracle Cards

Saints & Angels Oracle Cards

Magical Unicorns Oracle Cards

Goddess Guidance Oracle Cards

Archangel Oracle Cards

Magical Mermaids and Dolphins Oracle Cards

Messages from Your Angels Oracle Cards

Healing with the Fairies Oracle Cards

Healing with the Angels Oracle Cards

All of the above are available at your local bookstore, or may be ordered by visiting Hay House USA: www.hayhouse.com®; Hay House Australia: www.hayhouse.com.au; Hay House UK: www.hayhouse.co.uk; Hay House South Africa: www.hayhouse.co.za; Hay House India: www.hayhouse.co.in

Doreen's website: www.AngelTherapy.com

Don't
Let Anything
Dull Your
Sparkle

HOW TO BREAK FREE OF
NEGATIVITY & DRAMA

Doreen Virtue

HAY HOUSE, INC.
Carlsbad, California • New York City
London • Sydney • Johannesburg
Vancouver • New Delhi

Published and distributed in the United States by: Hay House, Inc.: www
.hayhouse.com® • *Published and distributed in Australia by:* Hay House
Australia Pty. Ltd.: www.hayhouse.com.au • *Published and distributed in the
United Kingdom by:* Hay House UK, Ltd.: www.hayhouse.co.uk • *Published
and distributed in the Republic of South Africa by:* Hay House SA (Pty), Ltd.:
www.hayhouse.co.za • *Distributed in Canada by:* Raincoast Books: www
.raincoast.com • *Published in India by:* Hay House Publishers India: www
.hayhouse.co.in

Interior design: Jenny Richards

The author of this book does not dispense medical advice or prescribe the
use of any technique as a form of treatment for physical, emotional, or medical problems without the advice of a physician, either directly or indirectly.
The intent of the author is only to offer information of a general nature to
help you in your quest for emotional and spiritual well-being. In the event
you use any of the information in this book for yourself, the author and the
publisher assume no responsibility for your actions.

The Library of Congress has cataloged the earlier edition as follows:

Virtue, Doreen, date.

Don't let anything dull your sparkle : how to break free of negativity and
drama / Doreen Virtue.

pages cm

Includes bibliographical references and index.

ISBN 978-1-4019-4627-2 (hardback)

1. Mind and body. 2. Spirituality. I. Title.

BF161.V573 2015

158.2--dc23

2015007080

Tradepaper ISBN: 978-1-4019-4628-9

10 9 8 7 6 5 4 3 2

1st edition, September 2015
2nd edition, February 2017

Printed in the United States of America

Contents

Preface

I'm known as an author of spiritual books and card decks. Although I studied and practiced psychology for years, I've been focused upon spirituality even longer.

This book was born of a spiritual experience in which I received a surprising inner message.

The inner message came when I was in San Francisco as part of a book tour. After 25 years on the road, I was feeling burned-out with travel. I loved teaching and meeting audiences, but getting to each city had become a major drag. I'd grown highly sensitized to things like the intensity of airport security stations, urban traffic and noise, air pollution, and frantic travel schedules. In addition, it was difficult to maintain my self-care routine on the road.

I wanted to stop touring, but it was the only way that I knew of to teach about my books. It was a career habit. Still, I was stressed-out from traveling, and it was getting to me.

Then it happened: I hit bottom with the stress. I was at the airport on my way to San Francisco. I'd just taught a workshop in Toronto during one of its snowy winter weekends. I was feeling cold and tired.

When I checked in at the Toronto airport, the airline representative told me that I'd been randomly selected for extra security-measure screenings. I'd have to go through a manual pat-down and additional x-ray scans! She handed me my boarding pass, which was prominently marked with the letters *SSSS,* a code for extra airport screening.

I began to cry with frustration. Usually, I could muster up a positive way to deal with airport security, such as prayer, engaging the security officers in conversation, or reminding myself that security was a measure to keep all passengers safe. But unbeknownst to me at the time, my diet, life stress, and unresolved traumas from my past had maxed me out to the point where I wasn't able to access my normal positive coping strategies.

The thought of undergoing additional security screening pushed me over the edge, and I was in tears of anguish. I loved writing and teaching, but the constant travel felt like I was trapped on a treadmill with no way off.

When I arrived in San Francisco on what seemed to be an extra-long flight, I decided that—no matter what the consequences—I had to stop traveling.

Then, the next day as I was walked along Post Street in Union Square, I heard the inner message that is the basis of this book. It was one sentence, which was so profound and rang so true that I was stopped in my tracks in front of the Tiffany store so that I could write it down:

"The reason why you and so many people are experiencing life drama is because you're addicted to histamine."

I heard this message as clearly as if another person was talking with me (which is the usual way I've received spiritual messages since childhood). Now, lest you think I was having auditory hallucinations, please know that my master's program in counseling psychology at Chapman University required all students to undergo a battery of psychological screening tests. I passed all of these tests and received my degree.

Researcher D. J. West gave this definition of the difference between a hallucination and a true psychic experience:

> Pathological hallucinations tend to keep to certain rather rigid patterns, to occur repeatedly during a manifest illness but not at other times, and to be accompanied by other symptoms and particularly by disturbances of consciousness and loss of awareness of the normal surroundings. The spontaneous psychic experience is more often an isolated event disconnected from any illness or known disturbance and definitely not accompanied by any loss of contact with normal surroundings. (West 1960)

Well, I definitely was in contact with my surroundings when I heard the message. I've also been 100 percent sober since 2003, so it wasn't a product of intoxication.

Studies show that the difference between an auditory hallucination and a true psychic experience is that the former is negative or ego based, and the latter is positive. And this was a *positive* message.

There was an *Aha!* sensation accompanying this message, but I didn't yet know the scope of its impact. I was somewhat familiar with the physiology of histamine. Intuitively, I felt that the words were pointing to my addictive cycle with histamine, produced by life stress and drama.

So, I wrote down the message and even posted it in my daily blog on Facebook. But then I forgot about it, until happenstance (which felt like Divine intervention) had the old quote I'd written on Facebook pop up one day.

That's when I began researching the addiction to histamine, and I was blown away by what I found! I realized that my meltdown at the Toronto airport was largely a buildup of the effects of my eating a high-histamine diet, being overwhelmed with stress (which increases histamine levels), and not taking the time to face and deal with past traumas I'd experienced.

Ironically, as an addictions and eating disorder therapist, I'd studied and treated trauma for decades. My doctoral dissertation was on the link between child abuse and the development of addictions, which later became the basis for my book about addiction and eating disorders called *Losing Your Pounds of Pain*. I'd attended workshops given by the pioneers of trauma research, including Drs. Peter Levine and Bessel van der Kolk.

I'd even remarked to a fellow psychotherapist that Dr. Levine's descriptions of trauma sounded like my own wounds. My colleague promptly scolded me for even considering that I might have experienced a trauma, since I hadn't been to war or been abused as a child (the two types of trauma most often connected to post-traumatic stress disorder). He berated me for using the term *trauma* lightly.

So I shrunk into a shell of apologies (probably *because* of the trauma I'd experienced) and decided that he must have been right. Since my traumas didn't involve child abuse or combat, I dismissed them. I overlooked the impact that these painful experiences had on my life.

After conducting the research for this book, though, I discovered that the definition of trauma is quite broad, and it turns out to include any situation where we feel horrified, helpless, or intensely fearful that we'll lose our lives. My experiences *were* traumatic by these definitions, and they did reorganize my body and brain chemistry, as well as leave me with psychological scars. I wasn't using the term *trauma* lightly at all, according to the research I studied. This was real trauma, for a lot of us.

My dismissing my feelings shows the level of denial that can block trauma recovery. Even with my clinical background, I didn't recognize my own post-trauma symptoms and had minimized the impact of what I'd endured. My colleague was also in denial, perhaps because he wasn't willing to face his own traumas.

Based upon my findings, I began to work on myself. I followed every recommendation for trauma healing you'll read about in this book, and found that it helped a lot.

At first, like a lot of trauma survivors, I was impatient and wanted immediate results. Once I caught myself in this behavior, I realized that it takes consistent commitment to heal patterns. After three or four months, I noticed a huge positive shift within myself. I felt a new level of happiness and contentment that I hadn't even known existed. I finally understood how my old trauma patterns had attracted drama in my present life. Once I saw this dynamic, I made a conscious decision to "Drama Detox," and the patterns faded away.

To my delight, the emotional detox healed me physically as well, as bloating and itchy skin symptoms I'd experienced also disappeared. I could see my cheekbones again! Following the methods you'll read about in this book also helped me transition my career smoothly. Friends remarked that I looked years younger, and I *felt* that way. A warm peacefulness in my heart replaced the gripping stress I'd become accustomed to.

I'm very excited to share what I've found with you, because I know it will positively change *your* life, too!

With love,

Doreen Virtue

PART I

The Science of "Sparkle"

Recovering Your Sparkle

If . . .

* you're stressed-out and tired

* you're overwhelmed by your sensitivity

* you don't feel good about yourself

* you push yourself to go faster

* you're forgetful and can't focus

* there's too much drama and negativity in your life

* your relationships are difficult

* your body isn't cooperating

* you're experiencing burnout in your career

. . . then it's time to recover your sparkle!

In this book, we'll explore how sensitive people like you are affected by negativity, drama, and trauma. You'll learn how your brain and hormonal-chemistry balance have been altered by your life's events. You'll also find out why you can't continue pushing yourself to go faster and do more.

This is a book about the science and spirituality of "sparkle." You'll read about scientific studies that show why our sparkle—our joy, inner peace, health, ability to focus, motivation, and happiness—dulls . . . and how to reignite it. To make the book more pleasant and readable, I've summarized the research. I could easily write about every cellular response to stress, but that could be stressful for you to wade through! So, this book is more narrative than clinical.

Because the literature shows that our short attention span is related to our drama-, stress-, and trauma-filled lifestyle, I've also avoided footnotes and numerical citations of studies. (Occasionally I've included references in parentheses to entries in the Bibliography.) My prayer is that you'll read the entire book, because each page contains important information. So, I've worked to make this book an effortless and enjoyable read.

The research you'll read about helps explain *why* your life is the way that it is. It's a relief to recognize the reason behind toxic patterns. It's wonderful to be aware of yourself and your inner processes. Suddenly, the world makes sense and you understand yourself.

You'll see how traumas you've experienced or witnessed have changed your brain and body chemistry. I have *not* included any details about traumas that I or others have endured. Studies show that we can become traumatized by hearing about another person's trauma. So I don't want to add to yours by describing mine. That way, you can relax and turn the pages of the book, reassured that it's safe and gentle.

I believe that God created you—and all of us—with an inner light. A glow. After all, we were all made in the image and likeness of God, and God is light. You're still sparkly, but like a lightbulb covered in dust, you might not feel or appear radiant. If you don't feel happy or excited about life right now, it means that your sparkle has been hidden.

Fortunately, there are answers and solutions, and the first step is to recognize your patterns. This is a book about how to discover those patterns—to help you feel happy and enthused about life. Know that God's glowing light within you can never be extinguished, soiled, or diminished.

According to the American Psychological Association (APA), there's a significant rise in the numbers of adults and children with increased stress levels. Adults report being stressed mainly about money, jobs, and the economy. The majority also report that they don't have enough time or motivation for self-care to remedy their stress levels. In children, elevated stress levels are correlated with being overweight, perhaps because they are stress-eating.

Some of these patterns may be biologically driven. For example, if you've experienced any form of mistreatment—physical or emotional abuse, neglect, bullying, and so on—or other life trauma, then your brain-chemical and hormone patterns are likely affecting your health, energy levels, and personality. This is especially true if you experienced intense fear, helplessness, or horror during the trauma.

The post-traumatic changes in your brain and adrenals may have addicted you to drama and negativity. Your body and brain go beyond homeostasis to a new state called *allostasis,* which means a physical reorganization of your chemistry and wiring, leading to specific behaviors following a trauma.

What may surprise you while reading this book is that your experiences with negativity and drama can be highly addictive patterns, with a physiological basis. That's right: your brain and body may be *hooked* on stressful experiences that dull your light. This isn't to blame anyone who's stuck in negativity, but rather is information to help you recognize and heal damaging patterns.

You'll also learn why drama, stress, and pushing yourself beyond your limits is dangerously unhealthy physically, mentally, and emotionally.

If that's not enough, stress and drama can cause weight issues. Our ancient instincts respond to stress by storing fat, because of unconscious fears that starvation may follow periods of drama. Additionally, our appetite for junk food increases. Under stress, we tend to choose foods that lead to water-weight gain and bloating.

In Part I, we'll delve into the ways in which your body—including your health, weight, appetite, and comfort levels—is affected by stress. Some of this material is clinical, but it's worth taking the time to at least skim through it. You'll find answers as to the question of why you act the way you do in this part of the book. Solutions to stress and drama are presented in Parts II and III.

CHAPTER ONE

Drama, Trauma, and Stress

I have a confession to make: prior to researching and writing this book, I sometimes judged those whose lives were continuously filled with drama.

But now, after completing *Don't Let Anything Dull Your Sparkle,* I have the same compassion for the people I once referred to as "drama queens" as I do for alcoholics, compulsive overeaters, and drug addicts. In fact, this book has helped me become more patient with *everyone* I meet, because I realize that most (if not all) of us are dealing with the aftermath of personal and global traumas.

That's because there's a real physiological basis to drama addiction. Behind every highly dramatic person lurks an unresolved trauma. Drama is his or her way of asking for love, and begging for help and understanding.

> BEHIND EVERY HIGHLY DRAMATIC PERSON LURKS AN UN-
> RESOLVED TRAUMA. DRAMA IS HIS OR HER WAY OF ASKING
> FOR LOVE, AND BEGGING FOR HELP AND UNDERSTANDING.

Here's what I've learned in researching and writing this book: we're collectively suffering from *trauma sickness,* which is fueling our appetite for drama.

Virtually everyone on this planet has been touched by trauma, especially secondary trauma from watching too many news clips of horrors and tragedy. Trauma is also the reason why we're addicted to reality television, celebrity gossip, frightening movies, and dramatic friends. Unhealed trauma is behind our health, weight, addiction, sleep, and relationship issues.

Perhaps most tragically, unhealed trauma interferes with us carrying out our Divine life purpose. Fears and insecurities can cause us to second-guess our inner guidance. Addictions from unhealed trauma can block us from clearly hearing the voice of God.

We were created to be shining examples of the joy and love of God. In fact, having a peaceful and open heart is one of the greatest ways we contribute to peace on earth.

Fortunately, we can heal from trauma and get on with our life—and our purpose.

Your Body Stores Traumatic Memories

Psychology and psychiatry once focused solely upon how the *mind* was affected by stress, drama, and trauma. Today, research has overwhelmingly shown that the *body* reacts, and changes in response, to life events. The key to healing from trauma and regaining our sparkle in life lies in listening to our bodies' calls for help.

> THE KEY TO HEALING FROM TRAUMA AND REGAINING OUR SPARKLE IN LIFE LIES IN LISTENING TO OUR BODIES' CALLS FOR HELP.

When I was the director of an all-women psychiatric unit called WomanKind at Cumberland Hall Hospital in Nashville, Tennessee, we had a massage therapist on staff who specialized in trauma healing, helping patients release trauma stored in their cells. Very often, patients who were blocked during talk therapy would get insights and catharsis during the trauma-specific massage sessions.

The Link Between Drama and Trauma

Difficult situations and challenging relationships often involve drama. *Drama* is defined as stressful circumstances, patterns, or relationships that *seem* to be out of your control. If drama happens continually in your life, your past traumas are probably the reason why.

Trauma is a situation that causes such great pain (emotionally, cognitively, and/or physically) that it shatters your sense of safety. Post-traumatic symptoms are more likely to occur in people who experience intense fear, helplessness, or horror during the trauma.

The words *drama* and *trauma* both have their roots in ancient Greece:

✳ *Drama* comes from the verb *dran,* which meant "to act" or "to do," and referred literally to theatrical productions. In a way, our modern definition is similar, except it now refers to the theater of real life. When a movie is called a "drama," that usually means we'll witness emotionally painful scenes.

✳ *Trauma* in the original Greek meant "wound," "hurt," or "defeat." Today, we usually think of trauma as a physical injury that brings a person to the hospital emergency room. However, many traumas injure the mind and emotions. This is especially true if you've had repeated traumas in your life.

In many cases, the person faces the threat of death. Examples include (but aren't limited to) vehicular accidents, child abuse, natural disasters, war, serious illness, the sudden and unexpected death of a loved one, or a crime incident.

Trauma reorganizes your brain patterns, which can make you more prone to reexperiencing trauma and drama. When this occurs, life can feel like a surreal movie. You don't feel like your real self, and you certainly don't feel like you're the director of the movie, either. Unhealed trauma can make us feel like we are victims of outside forces beyond our control.

Tallying Up Your Drama

Drama, a secondary pattern following trauma, is a form of self-sabotage and self-punishment that is highly addictive. Even if you protest that you can't stand drama, there are "secondary gain" rewards of involving yourself in dramatic situations and relationships, such as:

✳ Receiving sympathy and other forms of attention from others

✳ Focusing upon someone else's issues instead of your own

✳ Giving yourself a great excuse to procrastinate

✳ Feeling needed, either by rescuing others or being rescued

Drama is an unfortunate part of "revictimization" (repeated traumas), a frequent phenomenon in those who've been traumatized. We'll unravel this concept in the next chapter and give solutions throughout this book.

First, let's assess your personal Drama Quotient to help answer these questions:

⁎ How much drama do you tolerate?

⁎ How much do you "hook into" other people's drama?

⁎ Do you know the difference between drama-based rescuing and genuinely helping someone in need?

⁎ Do you attract your own drama?

The following isn't a scientifically verified testing method, yet it's based upon scientific research about post-traumatic symptoms and the addiction to stress chemicals.

DRAMA QUOTIENT QUIZ

Answer "Yes" or "No" to each question:

1. I can't stand to be alone.

2. I would rather be with someone difficult than be alone.

3. I am usually attracted to people who have problems.

4. I've had more than one abusive romantic partner.

5. My childhood was painful.

6. I feel guilty much of the time.

7. I love reading magazines and online articles about celebrities.

8. In conversations, I seem to be the person who knows the most about the personal lives of celebrities.

9. I enjoy watching reality television shows.

10. My life seems to be "one thing after another."

11. My life could *be* a reality television show.

12. People love to tell me about their problems.

13. A high percentage of my day is spent helping other people.

14. Sometimes I wonder whether inner peace is a possibility or just a fairy tale.

15. Being bored is one of the worst things in the world.

16. My loved ones complain that I blow everything out of proportion.

17. I could be happy and successful if my family members would get their acts together.

18. I consider myself to be a very strong person, who can take on more than the average person.

19. I visit my family out of guilt and obligation, not out of a desire to see them.

20. I often regret ignoring my intuition.

21. I'm one of the hardest-working people I know.

22. When there's a big and tragic news story, I feel very upset.

23. After someone tells me their problems, I keep thinking about them.

24. It's difficult for me to concentrate.

25. I'm often forgetful.

26. To keep my energy going, I rely upon caffeine and/or sugar.

27. I often have cravings for fermented foods, such as vinegar and sharp cheese.

28. I relax by drinking a large glass of wine or other alcoholic beverage.

29. I am worried about the next big catastrophe in my life.

30. I have been abused, physically or emotionally.

31. I've experienced one or more traumatic events in my life.

32. When disaster strikes in the world, I obsessively read or watch news stories about it.

33. I sometimes feel that I'm not real, and that life is just a movie.

34. I feel spacey much of the time, like I'm outside my body.

35. My skin itches a lot.

36. I frequently feel bloated with water-weight gain.

Drama Quotient quiz tally:

— If you answered 27 or more questions with a Yes response: **You Are Highly Stressed.**

Your answers indicate that you may have experienced life trauma, and now find yourself in an addictive drama cycle. You have a deep need to be with other people; however, the people in your life have high-drama lives that are affecting you.

— If you answered between 18 and 26 questions with a Yes response: **You Are Stressed.**

Based upon your answers, you're probably feeling anxious and tense much of the time. Your lifestyle is high-stress and filled with drama at work and in your relationships.

— If you answered 9 to 17 questions with a Yes response: **You Are Somewhat Stressed.**

Your answers show that you have life stress; however, you've learned how to manage it in healthful ways.

— If you answered 8 or fewer questions with a Yes response: **You Sparkle!**

Congratulations! Assuming you answered truthfully—and you're aware of your true feelings—you've arranged your life so that you have minimal stress, and you are taking excellent care of yourself. Now, if you minimized your "Yeses" because you're not aware of your stress level, or perfectionism has you denying the truth about your life, you in fact have a higher Drama Quotient.

Your Drama Quotient is your willingness to allow stress to rule your life. As you'll read in this book, you *do* have the choice of whether you say yes or no to stress.

The Choices We Make

Some people believe that stress is something outside themselves that happens *to* them. Yet, once you reach adulthood and have the ability to make your own lifestyle choices, you really do have the option of a low-stress life.

If that possibility sounds boring or impossible, this is a sign of drama addiction.

Perhaps you're not a dramatic person yourself, but you may be attracted to people who are. If this is the case, you probably feel like your life is stalled, because you spend all your time putting out fires for those you love. You're waiting for the day when the people you care about have happy lives— so that you can get started with your own.

We often feel as if drama, like stress, is nothing of our own doing. There's a sense that drama happens *to* us, not *from* us. Certainly, there are instances when this is true, such as when a family member has multiple dramatic experiences.

However, there are other instances when clearly you are in charge, such as:

✳ Choosing friends or romantic partners who have high-drama personalities

✳ Focusing upon low-priority activities, instead of working on what matters to you

✳ Ignoring your inner knowingness, which is warning you to stay away from a person, behavior, or situation

✳ Spending more money than your budget allows

✳ Abusing substances that magnify your anxiety (for example, *stimulants,* including caffeine, nicotine, and sugar) or depression (for instance, *depressants,* including alcohol)

✳ Not planning ahead and facing an impossible deadline that has you racing against the clock

These are a few examples of how our personal choices can
increase the drama in our lives—and dull our sparkle! These are
all forms of self-sabotage.

This isn't to blame you (after all, blame never helps anyone or
anything). Instead, it's a call to engage in detective work to help
you recover your beautiful sparkle and everything that goes with
it: happiness, health, peace, abundance, and high self-esteem.

Your true self, as God originally created you, is peaceful and
peace-loving. Drama may temporarily feel exciting, but it's the
junk food of life experiences: not satisfying and definitely not
healthful.

You were created to live peacefully with a meaningful and
love-filled life. In spiritual truth, you don't want drama. You crave
stability and the feeling of security. That's why, in the next chapter, we'll discuss why drama is both repelling and appealing.

CHAPTER TWO

Why Drama Always Seems to Find You

I s your life like an ongoing drama, and you keep waiting for a peaceful moment to catch your breath?

If so, you, fortunately, hold the key to switch off all—or most—of that drama. But first, let's understand the basis of the drama-attraction cycle. After all, your soul is already peaceful and is trying to express and create a peaceful life for you.

Drama and Brain Chemistry

Our brains are remarkable, ingeniously creating chemicals to insulate and protect us from pain. The trouble is, some of these brain chemicals feel so good that they become addictive.

Let's go back to the beginning. Our brains were wired to help our ancestors survive. We developed the ability to notice when something dangerous or out of the ordinary was brewing. So, we're continually scanning our environment for unusual occurrences. It's a self-protective mechanism, alerting us whether we need to run away from or fight whatever we're facing. This is called the *fight-or-flight response.*

If you've had traumatic experiences where you've had to use your fight-or-flight response, your brain and body remembers this at a cellular and chemical level.

Likewise, if you were overwhelmed during a trauma, you may have reacted in a deer-in-the-headlights way. You froze in time, feeling helpless to save yourself. This freeze response is an ancient instinctive reaction in the face of overwhelming danger.

After the trauma, your body's emergency system may be stuck in the "on" mode. This results in you overreacting to everything as if it's an urgent matter. You panic when everything's really okay.

Psychotherapist Pete Walker, author of *Complex PTSD,* has expanded the view of fight, flight, and freeze reactions to include an additional trauma response, called *fawn.* Fawning is the action of trying to please or placate someone to stay safe and get your needs met.

So here are the four reactions to trauma:

✳ **Fight:** Fighting back and resisting the trauma.

✳ **Flight:** Running away from the trauma.

✳ **Freeze:** The equivalent of the possum "playing dead" to avoid detection and danger. This also includes dissociating your awareness so that you won't be as conscious of the pain.

✳ **Fawn:** Trying to comply with and please the people involved in the trauma (such as abusive parents).

The definition of *trauma* differs for everyone. What's traumatic to you may not be so to someone else.

Most researchers define *trauma* as an experience in which you believe you're going to lose your life, you feel completely helpless, or you're filled with horror. Trauma can be anything that suddenly and completely disorients and disorganizes you. It's an experience instilling mortal fear in you such that you no longer feel secure in the world.

As I touched on in the previous chapter, traumas may include:

※   The sudden and unexpected death of a loved one (including pets)

※   Divorce—your own, your parents', or other loved ones'

※   Abuse—physical or emotional (including neglect)

※   Major illness

※   Your life being threatened

※   Moving

※   An accident

※   Difficulty giving birth

※   Financial difficulties

※   Bullying and painful teasing

※   Breakup with friends

✳ Losing your job

✳ Riots and public disturbances

✳ Abusive relationships

✳ Losing all faith in God and/or religion

✳ Surgery

✳ Having an abortion

✳ Legal issues

✳ Imprisonment

✳ War or military service

✳ Losing your home

✳ Being a crime victim

✳ A natural disaster (earthquake, hurricane, flood, etc.)

✳ Experiencing or witnessing violence

✳ Anything that shook up your feelings of safety and predictability

The more traumas you've experienced, the more *hyper-vigilant* you become in scanning the horizon for danger. The ancient part of your brain that is built to notice unusual occurrences is stuck in the "on" position.

This means you're jumpy, nervous, worried, and anxious . . . waiting for the next trauma to occur. You expect danger to be lurking just around the corner, and it's difficult to concentrate on work, studies, or anything "ordinary." Meditating is also challenging when you're hypervigilant because your mind is noisy with endless fear-based chatter.

Your chronic anxiety wears on your nervous and immune systems, and reduces your happiness. By expecting the worst, you may unconsciously attract or even create it.

Researchers have found that those who have experienced trauma are much more reactive to stress than nontraumatized people. Once you've been traumatized . . .

✳ . . . situations that would seem minor to others are a big deal to you.

✳ . . . you have strong physical and emotional reactions, such as panic, anger, and fear.

✳ . . . your brain's arousal system is set perpetually to high alert (unless you take healthy steps, as you'll read about in this book).

Additionally, negativity may block you from noticing your intuition. We all have the ability to sense and avoid danger. So, even though you're hypervigilantly looking out for it, you may inadvertently keep experiencing traumas because you're disconnected from your own gut feelings, which would warn you away from dangerous situations.

The Addiction to Drama

Studies reported by Dr. Bessel van der Kolk (considered the granddaddy of trauma research) show that the body can adjust to its environment so that once-uncomfortable and dramatic situations become thrilling and pleasurable. He writes:

This gradual adjustment signals a new chemical balance has been established within the body. . . . Just as with drug addiction, we start to crave the activity and experience withdrawal when it's not available. In the long run people become more preoccupied with the pain of withdrawal than the activity itself. (van der Kolk 2014)

Gambling similarly becomes addictive because the brain's feel-good hormone dopamine is activated in uncertain situations. With gambling, you never know *when* pulling the handle of the slot machine will yield money and excitement. So you *keep* pulling that slot-machine arm.

We are always soul searching for the bliss and peace we felt in Heaven prior to our physical lifetime. Temporary highs such as addictions and drama can feel like the path to bliss . . . only to disappoint us when the high wears off. (In Heaven, however, the bliss is constant.)

Drama addiction is identical to gambling addiction in that dopamine is released in response to the anticipation of a possible reward. When there's a perception of danger, stress hormones create a pleasant buzz, too.

Addiction to Stress Hormones

If you grew up in a drama-filled home, this energy seems familiar and even comfortable. It's what you know, and you may even feel that you can control and predict it.

Some theorists believe that drama addiction stems from neglect in childhood. If the only way you received parental attention was by dramatically acting out, this pattern can continue into adulthood.

In addition, high-stress situations at home, school, and work create addictive hormone and brain-chemistry patterns. For example, if you pushed yourself to excel in school, your brain and body became accustomed to high levels of adrenaline, cortisol, and histamine.

Stress hormones are secreted in response to perceived danger. They give a high, with benefits such as clear thinking, increased energy, and even superstrength (we've all heard the stories of petite mothers who were able to lift an automobile to save their children).

These superhuman feelings become addictive in the same way that people begin to depend upon caffeine for daily energy. No one *needs* caffeine or adrenaline, but a belief to the contrary can create a psychological dependency, in addition to any physical cravings.

Those who become addicted to stress chemicals like adrenaline, cortisol, and histamine suffer withdrawal symptoms when life is calm and without danger. Boredom sets in, and they unconsciously shake things up with drama to elicit the adrenaline high.

Stress hormones are helpful in dangerous fight-or-flight situations, because they enable you to take quick and decisive lifesaving action. But if the hormones are flowing constantly because of a perception that life is *always* dangerous, the results can include immune-system stress, elevated blood pressure and heart rate, acne, digestion issues, obesity, and decreased libido.

Those with a stress-hormone addiction approach life as a dangerous challenge. They're constantly trying to beat the clock, go faster, accomplish more, and surpass the competition.

There are countless metabolic processes involved with stress responses. However, let's briefly review the three major stress hormones that negatively impact us. Here's a very simplified synopsis:

— **Adrenaline,** also known as epinephrine, is a hormone and neurotransmitter. It's produced by the adrenals, which are two thumb-size glands sitting atop the kidneys near the lower back. Adrenaline is produced in response to fear, triggering the sympathetic nervous system, which means it spurs the body into taking action to escape or fight the frightening adversary or challenge. Adrenaline makes the heart beat faster. However, too much adrenaline over time can lead to heart disease and heart failure.

— **Cortisol** is a steroidal hormone produced by the adrenals. In stressful situations, cortisol increases blood sugar for energy, suppresses the immune system, and ensures that consumed food is stored as fat around the stomach. This is a primal response to stress, because in ancient times, drama was often followed by famine. Cortisol also increases the appetite, especially for sugar. Excess cortisol decreases collagen production, which is why stress leads to wrinkles. It also contributes to obesity and osteoporosis.

A 2015 study found that those with post-traumatic symptoms showed an increase in memory functioning when their cortisol was elevated. The opposite is true for people without post-traumatic symptoms. *This may mean that those who've been traumatized become addicted to cortisol* because it boosts cognitive performance, at least in terms of memory.

Levels of cortisol and other stress hormones also increase in those who are in marriages characterized by negativity. This may create a drama addiction to marital arguing and conflict (along with decreased immune functioning and wound healing).

Several studies have examined the cortisol levels of those who've been traumatized. In a global review of all these studies conducted in 2006, it was found that people who've experienced trauma have lower cortisol levels in their bodies than the general population. In particular, females who've experienced physical-abuse trauma (including sexual abuse) have consistently lower levels of cortisol.

Although cortisol is an addictive stress hormone that contributes to overeating and other issues, having abnormally low levels is also unhealthy. So those with post-traumatic stress and low cortisol aren't receiving the hormone protection for their immune system. It's a balance, where you don't want your cortisol levels to be too high or too low.

— **Histamine** is a neurotransmitter produced by the mast cells and white blood cells, in response to allergens. The release of histamine triggers allergic reactions, such as swelling, bloating, hives, rash, runny nose, watery eyes, sneezing, and itching. Seasickness is also a product of high histamine levels.

Histamine isn't a bad guy, though, as it promotes wakefulness and alertness. However, if we produce or ingest too much histamine, we may experience insomnia and anxiety. Excessive histamine affects the lungs, so it can cause shortness of breath and trigger a panic attack. Hypervigilance, a post-traumatic symptom, is produced by excessive histamine as well.

Consuming a lot of sugar, chocolate, nicotine, caffeine, and other stimulants increases adrenaline, cortisol, and histamine production. Also involved with drama addiction are the feel-good body and brain chemicals *dopamine, serotonin,* and *oxytocin.* These chemicals' relationship to drama will be discussed throughout this book.

With all brain and body chemicals, it's about balance. Too much or too little of any chemical upsets the whole system.

Burnout Syndrome

Burnout syndrome refers to people who are suffering from long-term exhaustion, depression, and a reduced interest in their work or life in general.

Studies show that burnout raises your stress-hormone levels, which can affect your cardiovascular health and increase your body weight.

Those who experience burnout display a significant reduction in their short-term memory and attention span. We usually think of burnout as being career related, picturing a person who works long hours, who is only at his or her job for money and not personal passion, or who dislikes the competitiveness or politics at his or her workplace.

The model of this phenomenon put forth by Dr. Geri Puleo, a leading researcher on the topic, shows that those prone to burnout are the "star players" at the company. They are the people who excel, are driven, and volunteer for extra assignments. Then they become angry and frustrated when their efforts aren't sufficiently rewarded. This leads to apathy and a decreased enthusiasm about their work. The apathy is the precursor to burnout.

A major study of nurses found that those who had PTSD diagnoses were also prone to burnout syndrome. The reverse was not true (those who are burned-out do not necessarily have PTSD).

Sometimes burnout includes frustration and depression, where you feel burned-out about living with continual disappointments, often a result of unresolved trauma leading to a drama and stress addiction.

One study showed that having a spiritual belief system provides insulation against the development of burnout—something that the scientists call the "Mother Teresa effect" (Newmeyer et al. 2014). So you can avoid burnout and add to your career enjoyment by looking for meaningful ways to help and inspire others. You might, for example, organize a charitable event for your workplace. You can also simply strive to be a compassionate co-worker or an inspiring manager.

Hypervigilance

Those who experienced childhood abuse develop hypervigilance as a survival skill. Tuning in to Mom and Dad's mood allowed you to avoid provoking or intensifying their anger. An increase in histamine levels could also trigger hypervigilance. This gave rise to the "fawn" effect, discussed earlier, and you developed people-pleasing skills, where you used a false front to appease your parents.

PEOPLE-PLEASING

Those who grew up "walking on eggshells" to avoid family arguments have difficulty recognizing this tendency in adulthood. They tiptoe through their relationships to anxiously avoid the minefield of conflict. They're terrified that someone might be angry or disappointed with them. Their focus is on the other person's feelings more than on their own.

An external focus to pick up on others' moods is developed as a survival skill. Dr. Peter Levine describes how gazelles are alerted to danger if a single herd member is startled. When one runs from perceived danger, the rest of the herd follows. He surmises that humans are the same way.

Levine says that humans intuitively pick up on whether someone's in a bad mood. We instinctively avoid angry people because they could be attackers. We also unconsciously notice people whose body language shows they are afraid, because their fear is a signal that we should run from danger ourselves (Levine 2010).

So, noticing others' moods keeps us safe. Yet, it can also disconnect us from noticing our own thoughts, intuition, and feelings. We're so focused upon others that we don't ask ourselves, *How am I feeling right now?*

In addition, those who have an external focus are more likely to succumb to "learned helplessness." This is a mental state where you become depressed because you feel trapped, like there's no escape. Those who have an internal locus of control—where you believe that you are in charge of your destiny—are less likely to develop learned-helplessness-based depression.

BOREDOM

Hypervigilance also means that you become bored easily. A person who constantly scans the horizon for potential danger is alert to unusual conditions. Anything new is a sign that something's not right. You scan right past everything that's stable or commonplace.

So with hypervigilance, you're searching for novelty. When things stay the same, your vigilance isn't rewarded. You look and look for something out of the ordinary as a sign of danger, but all you see are the same situations you saw yesterday.

This is when boredom sets in, because all your hard work vigilantly scanning for danger isn't paying off. Boredom is part of drama addiction, and has its basis in being a trauma survivor. So, hypervigilance may cause you to shake things up so that you have something new to focus upon. When life seems to be sailing along too smoothly, you turn it upside down.

> BOREDOM IS PART OF DRAMA ADDICTION, AND HAS ITS BASIS IN BEING A TRAUMA SURVIVOR.

Difficulty Concentrating

Those who've been traumatized often have learning challenges, including trouble with memory and focus. Trauma survivors are easily distracted. They therefore have difficulty completing tasks.

Researchers believe that hyperarousal makes us less likely to notice or remember details. Our surroundings become a blur. In addition, constantly scanning the environment for something exciting or dangerous is distracting.

Difficulties with concentration are correlated with sleep impairment, especially insomnia, arising from hypervigilance. The insomniac person is always on alert, which increases his or her stress-hormone levels and heart rate, and turns on the sympathetic nervous system. One of the roles of histamine, released in response to stress, is to ensure that you're wide-awake. These processes make relaxation and sleep difficult.

ATTENTION DEFICIT FROM TRAUMA

There are many similarities between the diagnostic criteria for attention deficit disorder and post-traumatic stress disorder. Both involve learning and concentration difficulties, as well as restlessness, inattention, impulsivity, sleep disruption, poor memory, anger issues, impatience, addictions, anxiety, and low self-esteem.

The main difference is *hypervigilance,* which is unique to trauma survivors and isn't part of the attention-deficit behavior spectrum. Hypervigilance, you'll recall, is the process of constantly scanning the environment for possible danger.

Another distinction is the tendency toward flashbacks in those who've suffered a trauma . . . as they keep reliving it through sleeping and waking nightmares.

Most treatment plans for attention deficit never relate it to past trauma. Since the treatment of post-traumatic issues is different from that of attention deficit, it's important to be aware of the trauma history of the individual. In Part II of this book, you'll read the latest recommendations for treating attention-related post-traumatic issues.

Impulsivity and Addictions

The need for immediate gratification is prevalent in those who've been traumatized. There's an urgency to numb the pain, especially when the situation is viewed as a dangerous crisis (even if it's not in reality). *Every* problem seems like a dangerous crisis to trauma survivors, so they are often accused of overreacting.

Researchers find strong impulsive tendencies in trauma survivors, including overeating, binge eating, and the addictive use of alcohol and drugs. Impulsive shopping is also common in those who are trying to cover up their feelings and gain social approval with their purchases.

Tragically, impulsivity can lead to self-harm and suicide among trauma survivors. Researchers believe that self-harm is a way of expressing anger and pain. It's a cry for help from those who don't know how to directly ask for or accept it.

Revictimization

Unfortunately, research has verified that those who've been abused are more likely to be "revictimized" and suffer additional assaults. A study of abused and traumatized youths found that they were significantly more likely to experience subsequent abuse. This is especially true for children who

exhibit a lot of anger. One bright light in the study was that children with supportive friends were less likely to experience revictimization.

Stress and drama addiction dulls your sparkle, and we'll discuss effective ways for you to heal. For now, though, let's continue exploring this paradigm. If reading about these traumatic effects is triggering tension in you, please hang in there with me. I promise that help is on the way.

If this discussion makes you uncomfortable, take your time reading these passages. After all, if you have suffered a trauma, your hypervigilance may make it difficult for you to focus.

Hypervigilance is one of the symptoms of the very real syndrome called *post-traumatic stress disorder* or *post-traumatic stress reaction,* which we will examine in the next chapter.

CHAPTER THREE

Post–traumatic Stress Reaction

When we think of post-traumatic stress disorder (PTSD), we envision soldiers having nightmares about battle scenes. But that's just part of the PTSD spectrum. As we've discussed, each person's experience of trauma is different.

Most people are familiar with the term *PTSD*. However, I prefer a different one coined by some researchers *PTSR*, or *post-traumatic stress reaction*. After all, it's not a neurotic *disorder*—it's an understandable *reaction* to trauma. The word *disorder* implies that you're abnormal, which is a disempowering identification.

> It's not a *disorder*—it's an understandable *reaction* to trauma.

If you have post-traumatic stress symptoms, you're not broken and there's nothing wrong with you. You're adapting to and coping with overwhelming circumstances.

For that reason, I'll use the terms *post-traumatic stress reaction* and *PTSR*. If you have PTSR, you've developed a survival reaction based upon having experienced trauma.

In addition, studies show that you can develop *secondary traumatic stress* (STS) from listening to or witnessing traumatic events. So if your dad shared graphic details about his experiences in the war, for example, you may have STS as a result, especially if you obsessed about what it was like for him.

Similarly, children suffer secondary traumatic stress if their parent with PTSR is withdrawn, won't show affection or other emotions, or avoids leaving the house (all symptoms of PTSR).

Researchers have found symptoms in those who *watch* news reports or videos about terrorism, war, and natural disasters. So if you were glued to your television set watching the footage of the events of September 11 or some other disaster, you may have STS from that experience.

> RESEARCHERS HAVE FOUND EVIDENCE OF PTSR IN THOSE WHO *WATCH* NEWS REPORTS OR VIDEOS ABOUT TERRORISM, WAR, AND NATURAL DISASTERS.

Apparently the unconscious mind can't distinguish between a trauma happening to you or someone else. Studies show that our stress hormone, *cortisol,* increases in response to our watching emotionally painful movies. This underscores the importance of using discernment and balance when watching news, movies, or television.

Post-traumatic Symptoms

Many trauma survivors minimize what happened. "It wasn't *that* bad," you might tell yourself. This is called *avoidant coping,* which means that you try to avoid facing painful memories by minimizing the impact they had upon you.

Yet, if you have these symptoms, the truth is that the trauma *has* affected you . . . and there's hope for healing. You *can* get your sparkle back!

Here are the symptoms associated with trauma:

✳ Recurring nightmares or flashbacks (realistic memories) of the traumatic event or events (can be completely emotional "feeling" memories, or may contain sights, sounds, muscle memory physical sensations, and smells)

✳ The inability to suppress fear

✳ Becoming upset by something triggering painful memories

✳ Feeling emotionally numb and detached

✳ A loss of interest in activities and relationships you once cared about

✳ Depression

✳ Feeling unsafe

✳ Anxiety

✳ Irritability

✳   Panic

✳   Hyperarousal (feeling like everything's a crisis
     or emergency)

✳   Insomnia and sleep disturbances

✳   Difficulty concentrating

✳   Dissociation, where you feel like you're not in your
     body

✳   Memory loss

✳   Chronic relationship issues

✳   Addictions

✳   Obsessive-compulsive behaviors

These symptoms can be normal coping and grieving mechanisms in the short-term. However, if symptoms continue past one month, it's an indication of PTSR. Researchers say that women are twice as likely to develop PTSR and are especially susceptible if they've had a traumatic sexual experience.

To receive a clinical diagnosis of post-traumatic stress disorder, therapists use survey checklists such as the Post-traumatic Diagnostic Scale (PDS). The diagnosis of PTSD is warranted if patients had a traumatic experience in which they felt helpless or terrified *and* they are having nightmares, flashbacks, or re-experiencing the event; have felt isolated and been avoidant of their loved ones and usual routines; and feel more anxious and hypervigilant following the traumatic event.

According to one study: "Based on the 5th edition of the Diagnostic and Statistical Manual of Mental Disorders, there are 636,120 ways for an individual to qualify for a diagnosis of posttraumatic stress disorder (PTSD)" (DiMauro et al. 2014). Another study concluded that the majority of people will experience at least one trauma in their lives, and one-fourth of them will develop post-traumatic stress symptoms.

While all forms of trauma can be devastating, the resulting symptoms may differ.

Anxious and Dissociative PTSR

Scientists have found actual neurological differences in those with chronic flashbacks and other PTSR symptoms, as compared to those who haven't been traumatized. Instruments measuring brain function show that those with PTSR exhibit unusual activity in their right temporal lobe, the area believed to be associated with memories of traumatic situations.

Using brain-scanning imagery, scientists have discovered two different models of PTSR responses:

— **Anxious PTSR.** The first type of brain response is found in those who are chronically anxious and fearful following their trauma. This type of PTSR activates the limbic centers in the brain, associated with hypervigilance and anxious fears.

— **Dissociative PTSR.** In the second, less common type of PTSR brain response, those who are traumatized become dazed and dissociated. This coping mechanism includes:

✴ *Depersonalization* (feeling as if you aren't real). Splitting your consciousness as a way of escaping an inescapable trauma results in dissociation. Your awareness leaves your body so that you aren't as conscious of the suffering.

✳ *Derealization* (feeling as if the world isn't real). Deciding that the traumatic situation isn't really occurring also reduces the experience of pain. However, after the trauma, dissociation often continues. The result is someone who isn't fully engaged in here-and-now living.

Dissociative response is correlated with being more vulnerable to repeated traumatization, phobias, and suicidal ideation, as well as with borderline personality. We will discuss ways to heal from dissociation so that you can enjoy your present moments.

Most likely, you've met people with both forms of PTSR. The anxious ones are fidgety and frequently angry, and the dissociated ones are forgetful and spacey. Perhaps these characteristics even describe *you*. These are symptoms of being traumatized, and once they are recognized and understood, significant healing *can* occur.

PTSR's Effects on the Brain and Body

A chief indicator that someone has PTSR is an inability to suppress fear. *Impaired fear inhibition* means that you don't have the capacity to deal with fear as much as a non-PTSR-afflicted person. Fear gets to you on a deeper and more intense level. You have an overly active startle response and panic a lot, convinced that everything's a crisis.

> A chief indicator that someone has PTSR is an inability to suppress fear.

Brain

Trauma changes the brain's patterns so that it's constantly on high speed, with resulting anxiety and hyperarousal. The amygdala, or fear-response part of the brain, is affected by PTSR. The constant anxiety can wear you down and lead to depression and fatigue, in an extreme roller coaster of moods and energy levels.

Brain differences can also determine whether you're more vulnerable to developing PTSR in the first place. In studies of combat soldiers, those who developed PTSR had a significantly smaller hippocampus (that part of the brain involved with memory and orientation to the physical world), compared to those who did not develop PTSR.

Scientists wondered if PTSR *caused* the hippocampus to shrink or if having a smaller hippocampus makes you more susceptible to PTSR. So they did studies with identical twins, with one twin who'd been in the military and the other who hadn't (Gilbertson et al. 2002). In these twin studies, regardless of whether one twin had gone into combat or not, when PTSR was present, there was a significantly smaller hippocampus.

Studies have found atrophy (shrinkage) of the hippocampus in those who've endured long-term stress. Fortunately, the hippocampus may be restored once the stressor is removed, with the exception of those who experienced trauma as an infant.

So, trauma affects the hippocampus, and having a small hippocampus makes you more vulnerable to PTSR symptoms, as well as depression.

Additionally, those who were abused as children show genetic differences. Scientists have discovered that certain genes
are "switched off" in order to help the child endure being in
an abusive situation.

So, PTSR physiology is significantly different in adults who
endured child abuse, compared to those who did not but rather who developed PTSR in adulthood. Perhaps that's because
many adults have a greater sense of being able to escape abuse,
compared to children, who are trapped and dependent if the
abusers are their custodians.

Following a trauma at any age, there's a reduction in the
number of neural pathways between the limbic system (per-
taining to feelings) and the cortex system (managing thought
and cognition). So after being traumatized, you're less aware
of your feelings.

The brain *changes* as a survival mechanism . . . as a way of
helping shield us from painful trauma. Trouble arises, though,
when this mechanism keeps numbing us long after the trauma
is over.

BODY

Not healing post-trauma is unhealthy. Studies show that
those diagnosed with PTSD have abnormally high leukocyte,
lymphocyte, and T-cell counts, suggesting that trauma affects
the normal functioning of the immune system.

It's one more reason why it's essential to . . .

✳ . . . use discernment whenever you have the choice
to avoid additional trauma (such as watching films
about disasters).

✳ . . . distance yourself from drama-filled relationships.

✳ . . . take measures to heal any post-traumatic symptoms you may have developed.

Fortunately, you'll find research on effective healing measures in this book.

Complex PTSR or DESNOS

When someone experienced *ongoing* traumatic stress from which he or she couldn't escape, the individual may develop *complex post-traumatic stress disorder* (C-PTSD) or *complex post-traumatic stress reaction* (C-PTSR). The official psychiatric diagnosis is *disorder of extreme stress not otherwise specified* (DESNOS). Examples of ongoing trauma are children who are chronically abused (physically, verbally, and/or sexually) or neglected (physically or emotionally) and have nowhere else to go and no one to turn to.

These situations effect complex changes in the person's ability to cope. Trapped people usually suppress the rage toward their captors and turn it on themselves with self-destructive and emotionally numbing addictions. Complex trauma results in extremely low self-esteem, because the person generally feels shame about his or her experiences.

In addition, studies show that when someone age 11 or younger experiences ongoing trauma, he or she is more likely to develop complex post-traumatic stress issues. Those who face ongoing stress in adulthood (such as imprisonment, an abusive marriage, or a pressure-filled job) may also develop complex traumatic symptoms, but not as frequently as those who were traumatized in childhood.

Psychotherapist Pete Walker, author of *Complex PTSD,* has identified these prominent symptoms of ongoing trauma:

✳ **Emotional flashbacks:** Instead of visual memories, sudden regressions to the feeling states you experienced during your trauma.

✳ **Toxic shame:** An overwhelming sense of shame and self-disdain, brought on by chronic physical and verbal abuse.

Almost everyone has been touched by trauma—at least secondary trauma—given the way videos and photos of disastrous events immediately reach us on the Internet and TV.

The question is: *how has trauma affected you?* Not everyone develops post-traumatic symptoms, but for those who do, life becomes an endless loop of drama and stress.

In the next chapter, we'll look at ways in which your diet may be a factor in reviving or hindering your sparkle.

CHAPTER FOUR

Histamine Addiction and Intolerance

If you crave fermented foods like sour cream, cheese, balsamic vinegar, red wine, pickles, yogurt, and tofu, then you probably have a histamine intolerance . . . *and* an addiction to histamine.

Histamine is a neurotransmitter produced by your body's mast cells in response to allergens, cold weather, stress, drama, and trauma.

Histamine is also prevalent in most foods and beverages. But some are *very* high in it. Fermented foods, soy, alcohol, cured meats, aged cheeses, and vinegar are loaded with histamine.

Some foods don't contain a lot of histamine, but they are histamine releasers. That means that their presence is an irritant that triggers mast cells to release histamine in an allergic reaction. Other foods block the production or effectiveness of an enzyme called *diamine oxidase,* which metabolizes histamine. Such foods are called "DAO blockers."

Imagine that you have a bucket inside of you labeled Histamine Bucket. As long as you don't overfill it, you're fine. In fact, we need some histamine for our health.

But every time you encounter an allergen, such as certain chemicals or air pollution, or stressful situations, your histamine bucket fills up higher. If you lead a stress- and drama-filled life, your histamine bucket is probably pretty full.

Then, when you introduce foods containing high amounts of histamine, it begins overflowing. That's when you experience painful symptoms. Irregular heart rate, bloating, headaches, itchy skin, excessive perspiration, hot flashes, feeling cold all the time, and stuffy or runny nose are just a few symptoms of *histamine intolerance.*

So if your body's histamine bucket is already full because you're around pollen, dander, stress, drama, and other triggers, *plus* you consume a lot of soy, fermented foods, pickles, and alcohol, your histamine bucket will "run over." Many women develop histamine intolerance in menopause as well.

Histamine intolerance is different from an allergy, so it isn't detected in normal allergy-test panels. Some foods contain histamine, and some are called "histamine liberators," because they trigger the body's production of histamine. For those who are histamine intolerant, the results are the same with high-histamine and histamine-liberator foods. I trust the histamine food chart from Swiss Interest Group Histamine Intolerance (SIGHI). Their website is www.histaminintoleranz .ch/en/introduction.html, with information in German, English, and French.

Here are some of the foods and beverages high in histamine or which trigger histamine production (histamine liberators or DAO blockers):

Additives

Aged and cured meat

Alcohol (especially red wine)

Avocados

Bananas

Black tea

Cabbage and sauerkraut

Carob

Cheese

Chocolate

Cinnamon

Citrus

Coffee and caffeine

Cranberries

Dried fruits with sulfur, such as dates; dried, nonsulfured, unsugared mangoes and apples are okay.

Eggplant

Egg whites

Fermented foods

Food dye

Ketchup

Leftovers*

Mushrooms

Mustard

Nuts (except macadamias)

Papaya

Peaches

Pesticides and genetically modified foods (GMO or GE)

Pickles and pickled products

Pineapple

Preservatives

Seeds (except chia seeds)

Shellfish

Smoked fish

Soy and soy sauce

Spinach

Strawberries

Sugar, refined (honey and maple syrup are okay)

Sulfites

Tofu

Tomatoes

Vinegar

Wheat

Yeast

Yogurt

*The longer any food sits before being consumed (even if it's refrigerated), the more bacteria grow in it and the more histamine is produced.

Histamine and Food Addiction

If most of your favorite foods are on the high-histamine list, you're not alone. Many "comfort" foods are involved in the histamine allergy-addiction cycle. You see, we tend to binge-eat the foods that we're allergic to. In the same way, those who are allergic to alcohol tend to binge-drink. We crave the high of the chemicals within these foods and drinks, as well as those our bodies release in reaction to them.

> WE BINGE-EAT THE FOODS THAT WE'RE ALLERGIC TO.

The process works like this: Histamine is released in response to allergens. This increases your heart rate and has an adrenaline-like effect. Researchers have identified that the brain releases opioids (the addictive chemicals within heroin and morphine) when you digest high-fat and high-sugar foods. But then the feeling wears off, so you crave more of the food to achieve the same high.

If you're already producing a lot of histamine because of exposure to stress and pollution, then eating high-histamine foods leads to painful symptoms. Stuffy and runny noses, itchy skin, arrhythmia, and headaches are just a few of the issues arising from a high-histamine lifestyle.

Researchers are concluding that symptoms can be alleviated by reducing the histamine in your diet, as well as your stress levels. One study said: "the existence of histamine intolerance has been underestimated" (Maintz and Novak 2007).

Interestingly, a 20-year study of 4,000 binge eaters pinpointed the most "addictive foods": sugar, fat, flour, wheat, artificial sweeteners, and caffeine—*all foods that are high in histamine!*

Studies show that binge eaters, alcoholics, and drug addicts all suffer from a decrease in the number and sensitivity of dopamine D2 receptors. This research has led to the conclusion that addiction to food and other substances is an effort to increase the feel-good brain chemical dopamine. It's a hunger for happiness and a desire to sparkle.

Histamine Intolerance

Histamine intolerance is frequently a symptom of an overly stressed lifestyle, which leads you to binge on high-histamine foods and beverages to calm yourself.

Sometimes histamine intolerance is a result of medical conditions associated with diamine oxidase (DAO) inhibition. DAO is an enzyme that metabolizes histamine. Some medications block DAO release as well. You can buy DAO supplements to help with histamine processing. However, be aware that some are made from pigs.

Pea sprouts, pea seedlings, and pea-sprout powder are a natural vegan source of nutritional DAO. Although peas are moderately high in histamine, some people can tolerate them without symptoms. If you can do so, they are an excellent low-fat source of protein (8 grams per cup).

In the absence of a medical condition, those who suffer from histamine symptoms are dealing with a histamine overload: too much drama, too much alcohol, and too many fermented foods.

✳   ✳   ✳

Now that we've looked at the physical and psychological reactions to stress, drama, and trauma, let's look at *solutions*. In Part II of the book, we'll examine the healing methods that are supported by scientific studies and time-honored tradition. Now let's dive in together and recover your natural sparkle and joy for life.

PART II

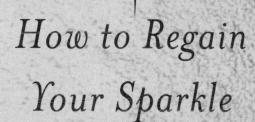

*How to Regain
Your Sparkle*

Yin and Yang Balance

Your sparkle is your inner glow; it is something that God created within you, which arises naturally from being enthusiastic about life. Think of a happy child, laughing and being him- or herself. That child sparkles, and so do *you* when you regain your inner glow.

The sparkle never goes away, but it can become dulled as the child's focus becomes more outwardly directed. As pressure builds to get good grades, to win approval, to compete for attention, and to fit in, the child's attention is less upon *How do I feel?* and more upon *How can I gain external rewards?* This is especially true if the child has experienced life trauma or has secondary traumatic stress from his or her parents' traumas.

As adults, we disconnect from awareness of our inner feedback that signals: *Warning—you are tired and stressed, and need to take a break!* We override these inner messages and keep pushing ourselves past tiredness, fears, and stress. That's when the stress hormones go into overdrive, affecting our weight, appetite, health, and personality.

The "Go Faster, Compete, Win at All Costs!" world belongs to *yang* energy, which is masculine. Yin energy is the feminine. Both are equally important for radiantly sparkling energy. The key is to understand the dark and the bright sides of yang and yin energy.

Every energy is part of an axis with opposites on either end. For example, "hungry" and "full" are the two poles of a continuum called *appetite*. "Hot" and "cold" are the ends of the *temperature* pole, and so on.

With masculine yang and feminine yin energies, the ends of the continuum are "bright" yang and "dark" yang, and "bright" yin and "dark" yin. "Bright" refers to the qualities that are generally considered positive, and "dark" the characteristics that are usually thought of as negative. "Bright" is life-affirming, and "dark" is troubled.

More Light Equals More Sparkle

Your inner sparkle is pure Divine light, which you were born with. To keep your sparkle shining brightly—and your yin and yang qualities "bright" and life-affirming—it's essential to immerse yourself in light energy.

That means avoiding people or situations that are primarily filled with dark yang or yin behaviors. (We'll delve further into relationships in Part III of this book.)

In the following chapters, let's discuss lifestyle methods to increase the amount of light in your life.

Bright Yang (Masculine) Qualities	Dark Yang (Masculine) Energy Aspects	Bright Yin (Feminine) Qualities	Dark Yin (Feminine) Energy Aspects
Motivated	Competitive	Nurturing	Jealous
Enthusiastic	Prone to lack mentality (believing there is not enough for everyone)	Sweet	Narcissistic
Helpful		Compassionate	Vain
Optimistic		Understanding	Insincere
Active		Joyful	Self-absorbed
Happy	Chronically angry	Forgiving	
Heroic		Attentive	Possessive
Successful	Quick-tempered	Gentle	Cold
Inspiring	Addicted	Receptive	Bitter
Honest	Bossy	Grateful	Uncaring
Of high morals	Rude	Soft	Superficial
Trustworthy	Pessimistic	Creative	Guilt-ridden
Respected as a leader	Thoughtless	Artistic	Entitled
	Restless	Loving	Nosy
	Exploitative	Peaceful	Self-conscious
	Violent	Generous	Nervous
	Sharp	Patient	Sour
	Blunt	Flexible	Anxious
	Blaming	Endowed with healing ability	Shallow
	Power-mongering		Insecure
	Jaded	Relationship-oriented	Passive or passive-aggressive
	Deceitful	Organized	Gossipy
	Punishing		Manipulative
	Sarcastic		Secretive
	Controlling		Perfectionistic
	Obsessed with acquiring		Isolated
	Critical		Irritable
	Harsh		
	Dishonest		

CHAPTER FIVE

De-stressing Your Life

Sometimes we have drama-filled lives because of fears that peace is boring. There's a lot of reinforcement in the media for this belief, with every television show and movie filled with conflict and drama.

I discovered this personally when TV producers at three different networks separately contacted me to be in a reality show about my work with angels. After they'd interview and film me and my family, though, each producer would say the same thing: "Your lives are too peaceful. No one would watch the show without drama and fighting. Peace is boring." One producer even asked us to pretend to argue, which we refused to do. With producers thinking this way, no wonder there's so much violence on television and in movies!

Why do we associate drama with entertainment? Well, it's because of the addiction to stress chemicals such as adrenaline, cortisol, and histamine. The heart-pounding excitement of stress makes us feel alive . . . for a few moments anyway, until our energy crashes afterward in the same way a sugar high is followed by an energy lull. Remember that studies show that these chemicals will be elevated even if we are watching the stressful situation happening to someone else, such as a dramatic television show or movie.

> THE HEART-POUNDING EXCITEMENT OF STRESS MAKES US FEEL ALIVE . . . FOR A FEW MOMENTS ANYWAY, UNTIL OUR ENERGY CRASHES AFTERWARD IN THE SAME WAY A SUGAR HIGH IS FOLLOWED BY AN ENERGY LULL.

Adrenaline, cortisol, and histamine give us a boost of energy, heightened awareness, and a heart-racing thrill. The trouble is, those bodily reactions are so toxic that they can lead to serious diseases and addictions. And if that's not enough, cortisol makes us insatiably hungry and gives us wrinkles—meaning that stress makes us look old and fat!

> CORTISOL MAKES US INSATIABLY HUNGRY AND GIVES US WRINKLES—MEANING THAT STRESS MAKES US LOOK OLD AND FAT!

We also equate drama with excitement because of conditioning from upbringings in stressful environments, including school classrooms. We often accept something we're comfortable with, even if it's an unhealthy condition, because it's predictable and we understand it.

As one who has lived both the crazy-stress and the tranquil, inner-peace lifestyles, I can tell you that the quieter excitement of peace yields more happiness. Being peaceful does not mean you sit around all day cross-legged with your eyes closed, repeating a mantra. You can be peaceful while engaged in very stimulating activities. It's just that you won't be driving yourself or other people crazy with nervous energy of fear or anxiety.

Have you ever spent time with a highly anxious person? It's draining and difficult! It's certainly not fun to be with someone who's expecting the worst to happen. And you don't want to *be* that person, either, for your own sake and that of the people who are with you.

From Self-Blame to Self-Worth

Feeling unworthy and unlovable and assuming that others will reject you are symptoms of trauma. This is especially true if you were abused, neglected, or rejected in early childhood.

The false assumption that you must have done something bad to deserve punishment leads to self-blame for the trauma. Of course this is an untrue and very sad belief. However, this is how trauma survivors organize their memories of their painful experiences.

These feelings can lead to *learned helplessness*, a psychological term for giving up and not even trying, which I touched upon briefly in Chapter 2. Learned helplessness can cause depression, where you stop caring what happens to you. You want to change your life, but it seems like a futile effort, because you doubt anything will change.

Here are some processes that may help:

✳ **One step at a time:** It's overwhelming to think of doing a lot, but it's manageable to think of doing one thing right now. Focus upon what you're doing in the moment, and the future will take care of itself.

✳ **Healing, not shaming:** Facing your issues is a way to heal them, not to beat yourself up over them. It's like peeling an onion: we all have issues we're working on, one layer at a time.

✳ **Detaching from diagnoses:** Avoid identifying yourself as a broken person. Instead of saying "I am anxious," use the more detached phrase "I am feeling anxious." The construction *I am* identifies you with the condition, which makes it more difficult to heal; while *I am feeling* signifies a temporary condition, not your identity.

From Pessimism to Optimism

Being pessimistic and expecting the worst is a post-traumatic symptom. It's our misguided way of shielding ourselves from future disappointments, by not even hoping or trying in the first place.

Pessimism gives you permission to not even attempt something fulfilling or healthful. You decide ahead of time that it's pointless to make an effort to lose weight, write that book, finish school, or follow your dreams. In fact, the favorite phrase of pessimism is "Dream on!"—as if it's crazy to dream about a better tomorrow. After all, if your yesterday was horribly painful, why *should* you expect today or tomorrow to be any better?

It's a negativity cycle, because if you don't attempt to improve your conditions, then nothing will improve . . . and, most likely, things will worsen due to your neglecting yourself.

We all have a Divine life purpose, which calls to you as inner pangs and pushes you to take positive action steps that will help others. For example, you may feel guided to be a healer, teacher, author, or artist. Yet following this guidance requires some semblance of self-confidence and believing in your abilities. Healing from trauma can increase your trust in your intuition and natural talents.

Some people think it's cool to be pessimistic, as it gives you a detached, I-don't-give-a-darn attitude. But these "cool" pessimists are left behind while the optimists go out into the world having fun and successful explorations. Many studies demonstrate the benefits of optimism, including increased well-being, greater ability to cope with illness, and a better quality of life.

To turn pessimism around requires that you have a glimmer of caring about yourself, your health, and your happiness. Think of a plant, which needs nutrients, water, sunshine, and loving care in order to grow. So do you! In fact, tending to a houseplant gets you in the healthful habit of caretaking, which can rub off on how you treat yourself.

Here are some ways to become more optimistic:

✳ Watch biographical movies about people who succeeded, despite all the odds against them.

✳ Write a list (or make one in your head) of the times when things *did* work out for you.

✳ Abstain from depressant chemicals, like alcohol, which dampen your enthusiasm for trying something positive and new.

✳ Avoid people who are chronically negative, as negativity is contagious.

✳ Be a "combination optimist/pessimist." You don't have to be optimistic about everything. A *more* positive outlook will help balance negativity.

✳ Pray for strength and healing. Studies show that spirituality is strongly correlated with healing from post-traumatic symptoms. Whether you choose a traditional religious route or a more personal spiritual path, developing a close bond, trust, and faith in your Creator can help you feel safe and secure.

✳ Make a point to initiate a friendship with someone who is consciously improving his or her life. Hang out with people who are accomplishing their dreams, and they'll take you along for the ride. Worried they won't want you around? Think again: successful people love to teach and mentor others, provided that you're kind and appreciative toward them in return.

✳ Start giving yourself appreciation and credit for your accomplishments, small and large. That's what optimists automatically do, and you can adopt this healthful habit.

How to Stop the Noise in Your Head

Negative chatter in your mind can drive you to addictions in an attempt to quiet the noise. Mind chatter is an inner form of drama. Some people use extra noise, such as loud music, in an attempt to muffle their mind chatter.

However, loud music (especially if it has aggressive lyrics) only increases thoughts and feelings of fear, anger, anxiety, and paranoia. Quiet music—which is usually labeled "meditation," "relaxation," "nature," "spa," or "yoga" music—mutes noisy chatter, and allows you to focus upon the priority at hand.

One study found that meditation music lowered cortisol levels while participants engaged in a stressful task. In the same study, those who listened to heavy-metal music had increased cortisol.

You may wonder: *But won't I fall asleep and be unproductive if I'm listening to meditation music?* This question represents the voice of the fearful mind speaking, because that part of the traumatized mind is afraid of being calm. It believes that fear keeps you safe because your guard is always up, on the lookout for danger.

So the fearful mind conjures all sorts of violent future possibilities and things to worry about. The fearful mind—sometimes referred to as the "ego"—believes that hypervigilance is the way to be prepared for inevitable disaster. This is the same mind-set that drives a fascination with violent scenes in movies, shows, and games . . . and in reality.

The fearful mind convinces you to identify the bad guys and what they're up to so you won't be a victim of their plots. The fearful mind also obsesses about news stories of terrorism, accidents, and plagues, and whispers to you: *This could happen to you, too.*

Having fights in your mind or imagining aggressive encounters with others or violent scenes isn't a *flashback*; it's a *flash-forward*, where you're expecting the future to be just as violent as—or *more* violent than—your past.

> BEING AFRAID OF THE FUTURE ISN'T A POST-TRAUMATIC *FLASHBACK*. IT'S A *FLASH-FORWARD*, WHERE YOU'RE EXPECTING— AND POSSIBLY CREATING—A FUTURE THAT IS WORSE THAN YOUR PAST.

However, being guarded, hypervigilant, and paranoid is not the way to stay safe. Those fearful habits have actually stripped you of safety, because your mind has been hijacked by fear. Sure, your body is alive, but you aren't living life fully if you're obsessing day and night about bad things happening to you.

Fighting against fearful thoughts just pours gasoline upon the fire. Anything you *resist* does *persist*. Instead, go around, under, and over the fears by taking the proven measures outlined in this book, including the Drama Detox presented in the next section and the techniques in the following chapters. Scientific studies galore say that yoga, meditation, breathwork, essential oils, spirituality, eye movement desensitization and reprocessing (EMDR), and cognitive psychotherapy do reduce fearful ruminating.

And lest you worry that you'd have to do all of above simultaneously to improve your thought patterns—please know that you don't. Pretty much *any* steps you take in a positive and healthful direction will carry you further than stressing about doing *all* the steps, now and perfectly (which the perfectionistic fearful mind would convince you is necessary).

Going on a Drama Detox

The nice thing about a detox is that you can approach it as a temporary stopgap, so the tyranny of your fearful mind won't argue with you about giving up something addictive forever. After undergoing a detox, you'll have the mental and emotional strength to make it a lifelong commitment.

We associate the word *detox* with the elimination of harmful chemicals from our diet. Detox traditionally means abstaining from alcohol, cigarettes, sugar, coffee, and other drugs. Yet if you're addicted to your body's and brain's stress and pleasure chemistry, detoxing takes on a whole new meaning.

As you read in Part I, scientific studies demonstrate that cortisol, dopamine, histamine, and adrenaline are released during stressful situations. The more stressful—or dramatic—the situation, the more your body and brain are flooded with addictive chemicals.

We also know that your body has a tolerance for a certain amount of histamine. The analogy is a bucket that can only hold so much histamine before it overflows. The more stress and drama in your life, the fuller your histamine bucket. Pollution, chemicals, alcohol, caffeine, and pickled foods all add to the histamine bucket. When it overflows, uncomfortable allergic symptoms such as bloating, itching, runny nose, and irritability ensue.

So a Drama Detox really involves reducing your stress levels. Like any other form of detox, it entails consciously abstaining from your "drug of choice"—in this case, addictive drama. *You* already know the drama patterns triggering your stressful feelings.

THE 5 STEPS TO A DRAMA DETOX

1. Set a date when you'll begin your Drama Detox. Commit to it by writing it in ink on your physical calendar and by adding it to your online or cell-phone calendar.

2. Decide on the length of time for your Drama Detox. Be realistic so that you don't set yourself up for disappointment. A good detox period in the beginning is three days. If all goes well, you can increase the amount of time.

3. Make a list of all of the drama patterns you are willing to abstain from. For example, you may decide to abstain from one or more of these stressors:

✳ Watching stressful movies or television programs

✳ Reading stressful news stories

✳ Interacting with stressful online social-media "friends"

✳ Associating with people who trigger drama in you or near you

✳ Overspending (debt is stressful)

✳ Overfilling your schedule (being too busy is stressful)

✳ Abusing alcohol or drugs

✳ Playing violent video games

✳ Listening to aggressive music

✳ Consuming high-histamine foods and beverages

✳ Consuming caffeine, nicotine, or other anxiety-producing stimulants

✳ Saying yes when you really want to say no

✳ Procrastinating and getting behind schedule

✳ Reading celebrity-gossip magazines (they encourage the addiction to drama)

4. Once you begin your Drama Detox, take it one minute at a time. This means that you focus upon your behaviors in the present moment, instead of worrying how you will abstain tomorrow. You tell yourself: *Right this moment, I choose to abstain from* _____ [describe the stressor you're detoxing from]. Notice how you feel as you're detoxing compared with how you felt during dramatic moments.

5. Have alternative plans for those moments when you crave drama. Every addiction involves dealing with cravings in the beginning. To avoid a relapse, it's essential to have replacement healthful behaviors available, such as:

✳ Calling a trustworthy friend, counselor, or 12-step sponsor

✳ Journaling about your feelings in a diary or computer Word document (you can always erase it later for privacy)

✳ Trading stress for stretching (lie down on the floor with a yoga mat or towel, and turn on a free gentle yoga class on YouTube)

✳ Going outside for a nature walk, or gardening

✳ Cuddling with a pet

✳ Doing something artistic and creative

✳ Engaging in a spiritual practice (for example, prayer, meditation, or attending a spiritual gathering)

✳ Cleaning out clutter and donating unwanted goods

✳ Listening to relaxing music

✳ Taking a warm sea-salt bath

✳ Getting a massage

As you can see, there are many healthful replacements for drama—and they are more fun and satisfying than drama, too! Have patience with the process of replacing old unhealthful cravings with your new healthful lifestyle choices. Any progress you make in the direction of health is positive and something to feel very good about.

Post-traumatic Triggers

If something reminds you of a trauma, you're likely to get triggered. That's when you'll experience post-traumatic symptoms and lose your sense of self.

A trigger can be "generalized," meaning that something reminds you of the trauma, even though it wasn't specifically part of the trauma itself. As one study on traumatic triggers concluded, "the traumatic memory may be stored in such a way that neutral stimuli that only vaguely resemble some feature of the traumatic event are sufficient to trigger the memory" (Kostek et al. 2014).

It's important to know what your personal triggers are so that you can understand what's happening when your stress levels begin to escalate. Yet if you overfocus upon identifying your triggers, you can actually trigger additional emotional pain. So, please respect this balance for yourself.

Triggers can be external, such as something you see, smell, or hear that reminds you of the trauma. An external trigger could be a place or a person you associate with the trauma. It's best to avoid external triggers as much as you can while you're healing.

Triggers can also be internal, which usually means a feeling that reminds you of how you felt prior to or during the trauma. Triggers such as sadness, anger, fright, or loneliness may motivate you to use addictions to numb them.

Internal triggers can also be "thought patterns," where you believe that something negative is about to happen. For example, you may believe that people are angry with you (when they're not in reality). Your belief may be a trigger to act out in unhealthful ways. You can also unconsciously self-fulfill negative beliefs, and make your fears a reality.

Triggers are ingrained thought and feeling patterns (which can be visceral and involve your sense of smell). They bypass logic and go straight to the nervous system, which reacts as if the trauma was recurring right now. Sometimes the process is unconscious, but with effort, you can begin to notice the trigger patterns as a way of healing them.

Be aware of triggers, but don't go into fear mode about encountering them. Instead, memorize a list of healthful ways to deal with stress such as "Get up from my desk and walk around for ten minutes," or "Stretch my arms and back to release these feelings."

Beware of What-ifs

Sometimes we get stuck in an endless loop of thinking about the past because we're analyzing what happened. It's all too easy to ruminate about the trauma, wishing that we'd acted in a different way in order to create a different outcome.

Obsessing about "what-ifs" (*What if this had happened instead?*) is a form of self-blame and self-punishment that is unhelpful and unhealthful.

It's beneficial to learn from mistakes so they aren't repeated. But holding on to guilt and shame is not productive. Remember also that if you were abused as a child, you did nothing wrong to cause this. No child deserves to be abused, period.

Guilt is when you blame yourself for some action that you took or did not take. It is not the same as taking responsibility. Guilt is a pervasive belief and a feeling. Responsibility is a thought process and a conclusion.

Shame is when you feel that there's something inherently bad about you. You're embarrassed by your perceived shortcomings. If you feel ashamed, you may isolate yourself. You may expect to be rejected, so you don't even try to socialize.

Guilt and shame dull your sparkle. They take the brightness and color out of life. It's essential to replace them with more accurate and healthier self-perceptions.

> Guilt and shame dull your sparkle. They take the brightness and color out of life.

There's nothing wrong with you. If you made a mistake, there's no need to punish yourself on an ongoing basis. Besides, doing so won't *undo* the past. But what will help the present and future is your taking healthful action steps so that you can make a positive difference in your and others' lives.

Your Relationship with Time

One source of stress is the way in which you view and manage time. How often have you been upset because you're running late or behind on a deadline? Time pressure is a major source of stress. Chronic lateness can also lead to relationship arguments.

Your brain under stress is focused upon surviving and re-acting, and less focused upon planning and creating. With chronic stress, your brain learns—and is rewired—to be focused upon survival and reacting only. It has difficulty amping up the area devoted to devising plans for the future.

Constant time urgency takes a toll on your body, brain, *and* emotions. Here are some time-urgency patterns and ways to heal them:

— **Approval seeking:** A mind-set of *I must get everything done right now, or I will be in trouble or something bad will happen* comes from the desire to prove yourself or to appease a real or imaginary authority figure. Usually, this stems from a childhood where you were working overtime to gain parental acceptance. As an adult, you can transfer the desire to win out-side approval to a healthy desire to give *yourself* approval. And that comes from taking positive action steps, such as peaceful-ly working instead of frantically racing against the clock.

— **Forcing yourself:** If you find yourself starting a sentence with the words "I have to . . ." stop and question why you're doing what you're doing. Why are you forcing and pushing yourself? That's a sign that your soul is rejecting the activity, and it isn't healthy. Either meditate and get to the point where you are happy to engage in the activity, make changes with respect to *how* you engage in it (switching to a more enjoyable workout routine, for example), or stop doing it altogether.

— **Indecisiveness:** The thought *I can't decide whether to do* <u>*this*</u> *or do* <u>*that*</u> can make you feel stuck. The existential dilemma of having to make choices concerning how to spend time is the basis of internal struggles and angst. Remember that *not* making a decision is the same as making one . . . because if you aren't making a decision, you're *deciding* to stay in your present state. Sometimes life calls you to make a choice before you're ready. Do your best, and go for what your soul calls you to do.

— **Not planning ahead:** Part of drama addiction is procrastinating until an appointment or deadline is upon you. Do you wait until Christmas Eve to shop for gifts, or the night before a report is due to begin it? These are examples of needlessly stressing yourself. Planning ahead is a new habit that can substantially lower your stress levels. One way to plan is to break a big task down into small steps, and then schedule them into your calendar. This is the method I use to meet my writing deadlines.

— **Stressing to impress:** Are you working like crazy to make enough money to buy prestigious items? Who are you trying to impress? This unhealthy and stressful habit stems from a desire to be loved. However, if people like you for what you own, it's a hollow feeling. You desire and deserve to be loved for who you *are* . . . beginning with loving yourself for having a calmer, more peaceful schedule.

— **Being a martyr:** Do you feel resentful and irritable because you have to do all of the work? This is stressful and toxic, and a sign that you need to (a) look for ways to simplify your life so that you're not bemoaning how much you have to do, and/or (b) start delegating tasks and asking others to help you.

— **Focusing upon the future:** After a trauma, it's natural to worry whether something painful will recur. However, if you become obsessed with fear about possible future traumas, you'll lose the enjoyment of the moment. This is a part of post-traumatic dissociation, where you lose present awareness of yourself. A simple and effective method for reconnecting with the present is to do deep breathing. Inhale deeply, and then exhale completely. Notice your heart rate. Be aware of whether you're comfortable or not. What do you see and hear right now? Focusing upon present feelings and environmental cues helps center you in the here and now. This empowers you to feel more confident about your present *and* your future.

Stopping the Stress-Drama Cycle

Our sparkle dulls when we don't enjoy our own companionship. Taking good care of ourselves, by eating healthfully and doing yoga, helps us love and appreciate ourselves.

Self-care is essential, but if you don't value yourself, you may not make the time for yourself. That's okay. In the beginning, small steps will help.

For example, become aware of tension in your jaw, your shoulder, your stomach, or another part of your body. If you notice any stress-related tension, stop whatever you're doing, walk away, and engage in positive self-care behaviors.

The same applies if you feel your heart racing into stress-related panic mode. Stop whatever you're doing, walk away, and take a few minutes to do one or all of these positive self-care behaviors:

- ✳ Close your eyes, and deeply inhale and slowly exhale.

- ✳ If you have a spiritual or religious orientation, say a prayer.

- ✳ Stretch your arms or any other part of your body that feels tense.

- ✳ Journal your feelings and thoughts at this moment.

- ✳ Ask for a hug from a trusted person, or stroke your pet dog or cat.

- ✳ Pray for Divine intervention to turn your fears into faith.

If you're often anxious, it's likely a post-traumatic symptom. Diet can also increase anxiety, as we've discussed. Know that taking self-care steps such as these, or any listed throughout this book, can help you to regain your sparkle that comes from inner peace.

In the next chapters, we'll look at natural active coping measures that you can use to feel calmer and happier.

CHAPTER SIX

Eating to Regain Your Sparkle

Those who've experienced trauma are more likely to overeat, choose unhealthful snacks, and not exercise, according to scientific research. Plus, if they normally eat when they're nervous or emotional, then any stress in their lives can increase their appetite even more.

And in a cruel twist, as people gain weight, they're subjected to what scientists call "cyclic obesity/weight-based stigma" (COBWEBS). What this means is that an overweight person is judged, teased, excluded, and rejected for his or her size. The stress of social ostracism creates a cortisol response in the body. This hormone then increases appetite, and he or she eats more and gains additional weight. It's a cycle that can lead to loneliness, depression, agoraphobia, and illness.

Fortunately, the COBWEBS cycle *can* be recognized and healed.

Researchers have studied the link between post-traumatic stress reaction in teen and adult trauma survivors—including in those who've fought in wars—and having an increased appetite for unhealthy foods and vulnerability to substance abuse. For example, they found that only 12.5 percent of war veterans had a normal body weight. The others were all clinically or morbidly obese (Smith 2009).

Those who chronically overindulge in food, alcohol, or medication are often trauma survivors. As I mentioned, my doctoral dissertation and my book *Losing Your Pounds of Pain* focused on the link between childhood abuse and the development of an eating disorder.

In addition, those who experienced trauma often develop impulsivity. So they will eat, drink, and smoke impulsively instead of rationally considering the long-term consequences.

In those who are traumatized, some of the excess weight may be attributed to the stress-hormone and neurotransmitter response because stressed people binge on food to which they are allergic. The allergic cycle, in turn, causes them to be hungrier, feel more anxious, and experience bloating and weight gain. Chapter 4 discussed how certain foods contain a lot of histamine. To recap, these foods trigger allergic reactions in your body, particularly if you're under a lot of stress.

When you consume foods and beverages that you're allergic to, your body releases histamine—its defense against allergens—from your mast cells. The trouble is that histamine produces uncomfortable symptoms such as bloating, itchy skin, profuse sweating, hot flashes, runny or stuffy nose, and feeling cold all the time, as well as low blood pressure, arrhythmia, anxiety, and depression.

It's normal to gain weight and feel sick when you eat foods that you're allergic to. The good news is that most people feel healthy and lose excess weight when they eliminate allergens from their diet.

All foods contain some histamine, but when you consume a diet that's high in histamine or histamine-inducing foods, your body is overwhelmed. This is especially true if you have a stressful lifestyle, since stress produces histamine. We're naturally allergic to stress!

As you'll recall from this book's Preface, I was guided to adopt a low-histamine diet and lifestyle. So I decided to abstain from high-histamine food for 30 days to see how it felt. This dietary change definitely limited my eating choices. It also meant I had to forgo some of my favorite foods (which I had likely been bingeing on because of their histamine content).

Within two days of going "low-histamine," I felt a youthful energy and exuberance that I had never experienced before. I felt well. I felt happy. And I knew it was due to the low-histamine diet. Darn it! I had been hoping that this diet *wouldn't* work so that I could return to my old eating habits of pickled foods, vinegar dressing on spinach salad, organic tofu, and papaya.

But when each day I felt better than the day before, I realized that eating low-histamine would be my new way of life. There's evidence that you can slowly add back in foods containing histamine. But you cannot return to the old patterns of bingeing upon dietary histamine once you realize the vicious cycle behind these binges.

I notice that when I deviate and eat high-histamine foods, I become upset more easily and don't have the tolerance for stressful situations that I do when I'm eating low-histamine. This could be because, similar to caffeine, high-histamine foods increase heart rate. A social-psychology principle called *attribution* says that when your heart rate accelerates, you may attribute it to anger or upset. You assume that you're upset because your heart is racing, when it's really a chemical reaction. But because you believe you're upset, you begin to *feel* upset.

As a reminder, most high-histamine foods are pickled with vinegar, aged, or fermented. They aren't *fresh,* in other words.

Doesn't that description sound dark, knowing that the life force of the food has long gone?

Histamine foods have tastes that are on the chart of dark yang or yin qualities from the Introduction to Part II, such as being sour, sharp, bitter, and harsh. They aren't sparkly—that's for sure!

High-histamine foods are often processed. They barely resemble their natural origins, because they're aged and mixed with additives, preservatives, and pesticides.

Low-histamine foods, in contrast, are fresh and unprocessed. They're filled with light and life force. Their tastes are among the light yang and yin qualities, such as sweet, soft, and nurturing.

Most of the foods high in histamine, interestingly, are the ones that traditional Chinese medicine considers "hot"; this refers not to temperature, but to the hot reactions they create in the body. They heat up the body *too* much, though, if consumed in excess . . . especially if you're under a lot of stress. *Hot* reactions include profuse sweating and hot flashes, as well as hives and itching. "Hot" foods are considered yang.

Yin foods are considered cold or cool, not in temperature but in terms of how the body reacts to them. These are also correlated with the low-histamine foods.

Remember that the competitive, stressful work world is a yang energy, so you want to balance this with a yin diet and gentle yin activities. It's all about balance.

When you're feeling stressed, especially if you're experiencing the histamine symptoms outlined in this chapter and in Chapter 4, reduce or eliminate high-histamine foods such as:

✳ Aged or processed meats, poultry, or fish, especially shellfish, which is naturally high in histamine

✳ Soured and aged dairy products, such as sour cream, yogurt, and cheese

✳ Yeast products, especially those made with wheat

✳ Anything pickled in vinegar

✳ Red wine

✳ Anything fermented

✳ Processed soy products

✳ Additives and preservatives

You'll recall that there are a few naturally high-histamine foods: avocados, spinach, tomatoes, eggplant, chili peppers, strawberries, nuts (except for macadamias), seeds (except for chia), and papaya. These foods are inherently sharp, sour, or acidic. However, as I mentioned, the majority of high-histamine foods are processed. When I made the decision to eliminate processed foods from my diet, I lost ten pounds within two weeks, and my stomach flattened. Processed food is generally fattening!

It's interesting that a few of the high-histamine foods—tomato, eggplant, and peppers—are from the nightshade family of plants. That means they all contain glycoalkaloids and steroid alkaloids, which can trigger temporary experiences of muscular aches, pain, inflammation, and inhibited body movement in sensitive individuals.

In addition to the above, avoid anything containing pesticides. There's a reason why our bodies release histamine in an allergic reaction when we eat or drink something containing pesticides. After all, the suffix *-cide* means "to kill." How harsh and dark is that? There's no sparkle in that intention!

Genetically modified organisms (GMOs) or genetically engineered (GE) foods have pesticides built into them, so all GMO/GE foods have the potential to cause allergies. Pesticides and GMOs actually contribute to stress as the body struggles to fend off the poison. In addition, the histamine released by pesticides can increase bloating and weight. In other words, GMOs are fattening!

For that reason, it's best to eat organic, non-GMO foods. Some people worry about the cost of organics, but there are ways to manage this. Growing your own, shopping at the organic booths at farmers' markets, and joining an organic co-op are some options to economically add organics into your diet.

Most grocery-store managers will listen to consumer requests for new products, so you can also ask your local supermarket to start carrying frozen or fresh organic foods. When you consider the high cost of dealing with the symptoms that arise from histamine allergic reactions, you'll *save* money by avoiding pesticides.

A Note about Leftovers: The longer any food sits before being consumed (even if it's refrigerated), the more bacteria grow in it, and the more histamine is produced. To go ultra-low-histamine, only eat freshly made foods. This means cooking with portion control in mind. Frozen food seems to be the exception, as bacteria doesn't grow in ultra-cold settings.

High-Histamine Beverages

When it comes to regaining our sparkle, what we *drink* is just as important as what we *eat.* It's all about taking in more light, and staying away from darkness.

As with food, the fresher and more natural your beverage is, the better. So, fresh water (without additives such as fluoride) is a wonderful low-histamine beverage choice. Water is also absolutely vital, because histamine is released when the body is dehydrated.

JUICE

Citrus has some histamine in it, so those with low-stress lives can usually tolerate it. But if your life is hectic, it's best to lower your histamine quotient by steering clear of citrus. Anything sour tends to have histamine.

Apples are naturally low in histamine, so organic apple juice is a great beverage choice. It's easy to make apple juice by blending sliced organic apples with filtered water in your high-powered blender. As long as your apples are organic and non-GMO, you can leave them unpeeled while blending them. You can also use apples as a sweetening agent in your vegetable soups and other meals.

CAFFEINE, COCOA, AND ALCOHOL

Okay, let's bring up the addictive beverages that most commonly trigger histamine reactions. I realize that in all likelihood some of these are your favorites; however, it could be that you like them for the "histamine high" that they give to you. This high of boosted energy and pleasure is short-lived and is always followed by an energy crash, *plus* all the painful symptoms we've discussed.

Numerous studies show that traumatized people are significantly more likely to abuse alcohol and drugs. These studies have been conducted upon war veterans, women who've had abortions, abuse survivors, and those who've experienced natural disasters such as an earthquake. As trauma changes the brain chemistry and alters perception, sobriety can feel frightening and too intense.

There's a physical dependency upon coffee, cola, caffeinated tea, and alcohol, which stems from the body getting hooked on the chemical reaction triggered by the beverage, as well as a psychological dependency.

— With caffeine, the psychological dependency is that desire to push yourself to go faster, usually in a high-stress job that you don't really want to be in. Sometimes, people depend upon caffeine because they're competitive and want to work more hours to get ahead. Those who engage in the "fawn" response to trauma often use caffeine to push themselves in order to gain approval from others.

— With cacao (cocoa and mocha) and carob, which are high in histamine, there's a desire for fun, pleasure, and love. After all, chocolate contains phenylethylamine (PEA), the same chemical your brain produces when you're newly in love.

— Alcohol is high in histamine. Even the so-called low-histamine variety of wine still contains histamine! In addition, wine and ciders contain sulfites, which cause bloating and itching in sulfite-sensitive people. There's also a psychological dependency, such as relying upon alcohol to relax, sleep, and feel more comfortable in social situations.

Ironically, choosing high-histamine beverages to deal with stress actually *increases* your body's stress. Your stress hormones and neurotransmitters work overtime to fight off the allergens.

So whether the psychological dependency is related to a desire to unwind, go faster, have more fun, or feel love . . . these high-histamine beverages are artificial means to legitimate goals. There are natural methods to achieve all of these goals, as we'll explore in the next chapters. And with natural methods, the pleasurable feelings stay with you.

High-Stress Diet and Weight

When you regain your sparkle, you naturally lose excess weight. You look and feel much better by bringing more light into your life!

Stress hormones and a high-histamine diet lead to bloating, water retention, and weight gain. Scientists have pointed to extra fat around the stomach, in particular, as a consequence of a high-stress lifestyle.

As I've mentioned, the primitive part of the brain believes that stress is a sign of coming famine and deprivation. When we're stressed, the body increases its levels of neuropeptide y, which a 2011 University of Michigan study concluded restores calm after stressful events. Neuropeptide y also stimulates the appetite for carbohydrates, and keeps us feeling hungry even after we've eaten. Studies show that we will continue to be hungry six to eight hours after the stressful event, thanks to the increased neuropeptide y. If that's not enough, neuropeptide y also leads the body to store fat in the cells of the stomach, for a ready supply of energy.

A high-stress lifestyle leads us to binge on high-histamine food and beverages in our attempt to feel better. Unfortunately, the result is—you guessed it—weight gain, water retention, and bloating.

Those who are stressed may turn to coffee to keep their energy high. However, drinking five or more cups of coffee a day leads to weight gain and difficulty losing weight, according to researchers at University of Western Australia. The scientists were studying the beneficial effects of caffeine, but their research instead pointed to the link between caffeine and weight issues (Mubarak et al. 2013).

Studies show that caffeine boosts cortisol, which prompts the body to store food as fat, instead of burning it for fuel. Cortisol from consuming caffeine also elicits hunger.

In short, coffee is *not* the weight-loss tool it was once believed to be.

Sugar Cravings

Those who are stressed commonly crave sugary sweets. This is because of hypoglycemia (low blood sugar) associated with the overproduction of cortisol and the slow release of the body's own glucose.

Eating sugar or carbohydrates gives a temporary energy lift, but it's followed by another energy crash . . . usually in the afternoon.

The desire for sweet foods and beverages has been demonstrated in infants. Scientists believe that we have an innate appetite for sweetness because our ancestors used this sense to detect which fruit had ripened and was ready to eat. That's probably why it's healthier to satiate sweet cravings with ripe fruit, rather than processed sugar. Mangoes, which are a low-histamine fruit, are a very sweet natural snack. If you can't find them fresh in your area, you can usually buy organic dried mangoes or frozen organic mango chunks . . . without sugar or sulfites added.

Vitamin C

If you don't have enough vitamin C in your system, your body will compensate by increasing your serum histamine levels. So, it's important to boost your vitamin C intake if you are stressed and/or histamine intolerant. Vitamin C is a natural antihistamine.

We traditionally think of orange juice as a ready source of vitamin C. But since oranges are high in histamine, your vitamin C can come from other low-histamine sources such as:

✴ **Mango:** 60.1 milligrams per cup (cut pieces)

✴ **Kale:** 80.4 milligrams per cup

✴ **Broccoli:** 81.2 milligrams per cup

The recommended daily allowance of vitamin C per day is 90 milligrams for adult men and 75 milligrams for adult females (increased to 85 mg during pregnancy and 120 mg while breast feeding). You can see that eating a serving of broccoli, kale, and mango could easily meet these recommendations. Processing food by cooking, drying, canning, or freezing it does lower its vitamin C content.

You may also consider a vitamin C supplement. Just be sure to read the label to make certain that its source is organic and non-GMO. A lot of vitamin C supplements are made from conventional corn and contain pesticides and herbicides, which will increase your histamine levels and lead to undesirable symptoms.

Addictive Foods Are Binge Foods

The physiology of binge eating was explained in Chapter 4. But it's important to reiterate the bottom line: when you eat or drink something that you're allergic to, you tend to binge on it because allergens promote addictive stress hormones, including histamine.

So you may believe that high-histamine foods and beverages are your "favorites" just because you binge on them. *Bingeing* and *enjoying* are two entirely different processes, however:

✴ With *bingeing*, there's an urgency to shovel as much as you can into your mouth. There's a feeling that you can't get enough, or that someone might take the food or beverage away from you.

✴ In *enjoying* a meal, in contrast, you take your time and savor each bite or swallow.

Once you reduce or eliminate the foods and beverages you're allergic to, you'll find yourself enjoying meals more. They become more relaxed and less stressful.

And if you can reduce your stress levels, you may be able to introduce some of the histamine-containing foods and beverages back into your life. However, if you feel yourself losing control and bingeing, this is a sign that you aren't yet ready to consume that item.

Instead, you may want to try some environmental and natural remedies for stress relief—as discussed in the next chapters.

CHAPTER SEVEN

Your Sparkling Environment

In the previous chapter, we discussed how eating food with pesticides triggers the release of histamines, as the body tries to ward off the effects of ingesting poison. Yet it's also essential to reduce exposure to pesticides in general.

Several studies have found that pesticide exposure increases histamine, cortisol, and allergic reactions (Kido 2013, Ezemonye 2011, Sato 1998, Rohr 1985). Similarly, research has conclusively demonstrated that environmental chemicals—found in carpeting, dry cleaning, household cleaning supplies, cosmetics, clothing, bedding, and such—are toxic (Birnbaum 2013).

We don't want to live in fear of exposure to chemicals, as fear and stress are in themselves unhealthful, as we've been discussing. However, this chapter presents an overview of environmental factors that can trigger stress-hormone production and allergic reactions . . . along with some healthier alternatives for you. The more you can reduce your exposure to toxins, the more you naturally sparkle.

It's all about being aware of how *you* react, emotionally and physically, to your environment. Most important is cutting down on as many histamine inducers as you can during times of heightened life stress when your "histamine bucket" is already full. That means modifying or reducing your exposure to the following sources of environmental toxins:

Carpet Fumes

Instead of installing new carpets, which are loaded with toxic chemicals that emit fumes, try wood or bamboo flooring, or decorate with beautiful vintage rugs. New-carpeting fumes come from adhesives, foam cushions, and the anti-static and anti-stain chemical treatments. Studies show that these chemicals—which include *formaldehyde, urethane, methyl butane, acetate, styrene, toluene,* and *polypropylene*—can trigger histamine release and other allergic reactions in sensitive people (Tanaka 2014, Sakamoto 2012), in addition to being health hazards.

Paint Fumes

Traditional house paint contains toxic fumes known as *volatile organic compounds* (VOC), which trigger allergic reactions in sensitive people. It's also loaded with heavy metals, which increase histamine production and allergic reactions (Graevskaya 2003, Huszti 1995). Fortunately, healthier paint options, labeled *no-VOC* because they don't emit as many toxic fumes, are available now. However, these paints still do contain some chemicals. If you're painting in a room where infants or allergy-prone individuals will stay, look for organic, plant-based paints, which are virtually chemical-free.

Cleaning Supplies

One of the biggest sources of chemical toxicity comes from home cleaning supplies, which contain harsh ingredients that can be hazardous as well as allergy-producing. Fortunately, Mother Nature has provided us with organic essential oils, which disinfect and clean without harmful additives. I've used these oils as cleaners for years and can attest that they work— and make your home smell like a spa!

Simply purchase a heavy-duty spray bottle from a hardware store and add two tablespoons each of tea-tree, eucalyptus, and lavender oils and then fill with filtered water. You can buy organic essential oils in money-saving bulk quantities online or at health-food stores.

Laundry Detergents

A study found that conventional laundry soap and fabric-softener sheets emit more than 25 toxic chemicals from the dryer vent. These include *acetaldehyde* and *benzene,* known carcinogens that the U.S. Environmental Protection Agency says have no safe exposure levels (Steinemann 2011).

You can protect your health and reduce skin allergies by washing clothing, towels, and sheets with eco-friendly laundry soap. Or make your own from borax and washing soda— you can find many recipes for homemade laundry powder and soap online.

If you love the smell of a dryer sheet, it's healthful and easy to make your own by pouring lavender essential oil on washcloths and throwing them in the dryer with your clothing. I've done this for years and have never had any problems arise from the oil coming into direct contact with fabric.

Dry-Cleaning Chemicals

Along the same lines as laundry soap, dry cleaning involves harsh and toxic chemicals. "Wearing" these chemicals on dry-cleaned clothing puts them in direct contact with your pores and your nose in close proximity to the fumes.

The main chemical used for dry cleaning is called *tetrachloroethylene,* also known as *perchloroethylene,* or "perc." Perc has been classified by the U.S. Environmental Protection Agency as a "likely carcinogen" that can cause nerve and brain damage. Studies show that even a small amount of perc leads to elevated histamine levels and other allergic reactions (Seo 2008).

Fortunately, organic and eco-friendly dry cleaners are becoming more commonplace these days. The first thing you'll notice as you step into one of these forward-thinking shops is the absence of the fumes and smells associated with dry cleaning. When you get your clothing home, you'll continue to notice the positive difference of not smelling the dry-cleaning chemicals.

Plastics and BPA

An ingredient used for hardening in most plastics is called *bisphenol A* (BPA). Many studies show that BPA is a hormone disrupter that triggers the release of histamine. BPA consumption has been associated with the development of asthma, obesity, heart disease, and diabetes in adults and in children— including fetuses, who absorb BPA from their mother (Moon et al. 2015; O'Brien, Dolinoy, and Mancuso 2014; Nakajima, Goldblum, and Midoro-Horiuti 2012; Melzer et al. 2010).

You can reduce BPA exposure by limiting your contact with plastics. In particular, never drink water from plastic bottles, including those large plastic bottles commonly used in office water stations. Switch to lead-free glass bottles filled with filtered water, or choose a stainless-steel sports bottle. If you do use plastic drinking bottles, don't drink them after they've sat in a hot car (although most commercial plastic water bottles have already sat in the heat while being prepared for market). It's also essential to opt for BPA-free baby bottles, which are now readily available for sale.

BPA is released when plastic is heated, so never microwave plastic bowls. Consumer awareness of BPA is so high that many companies have created BPA-free plastic products, including sealable plastic bowls. A simple Internet search for "BPA-free bowls" will help you to locate them.

BPA also lines the metal of canned beans, vegetables, and so forth, with the exception of a few forward-thinking companies that proudly state on the label that their cans are BPA-free. This is one more reason to choose fresh foods.

BPA is also found on the paper receipts that are printed from cash registers. So if you're really trying to avoid BPA, don't touch receipts.

Toiletries and Cosmetics

There is little or no regulation over the chemicals allowed in toiletries and makeup, so it's "consumer beware"—especially if you're chemically sensitive. Products like antibacterial hand cleaner, shampoos, lotions, toothpaste, lipstick, hair color, and nail polish often contain toxic chemicals and heavy metals that can lead to allergic reactions, as well as be carcinogenic.

In addition, toiletries and cosmetics can contain several histamine-releasing substances—including cinnamaldehyde, balsam of peru, benzoates of any type, sulfites, and dyes—that cause contact allergies. (VanderEnde 2001, Schaubschläger 1991).

Your best bet is to read ingredient labels on everything you buy, including what you put on your skin. After all, each of your pores functions like a little mouth absorbing whatever you're rubbing on your skin. A good rule of thumb is: "If you wouldn't eat it, then don't put it on your skin."

You can find nontoxic and effective personal-care and beauty products at most health-food stores and online. An Internet search will also yield healthful recipes for homemade versions of deodorant, toothpaste, shaving cream, conditioner, and such.

I love the cosmetics database by the Environmental Working Group (ewg.org/skindeep), which allows you to type in the name of your personal-care and beauty products to find out if they are toxic or nontoxic, and why.

Clothing Dyes and Chemicals

Anything you wear needs to be nontoxic and as close to chemical-free as possible, and that includes your clothing. When I first began investigating the clothing–allergy link, I was shocked to find out how many chemicals were involved in the manufacturing process.

Clothing labeled anti-static, anti-cling, anti-shrink, flame-retardant, wrinkle-proof, waterproof, and so forth have been treated with formaldehyde, a highly toxic, carcinogenic chemical that increases histamine production and causes contact dermatitis and other allergic reactions (Tanaka 2014, Fujimaki 1992).

Clothing-dye colors are saturated with formaldehyde, also. Shockingly, most countries have no standards for acceptable chemicals in fabrics, even though they come in contact with us intimately and are used to clothe infants.

A 2007 New Zealand investigation of formaldehyde in children's clothing manufactured in China found up to 900 times the level considered "safe" (Clement 2011). Flame retardants on children's pajamas add even more chemical toxicity.

Cotton clothing is filled with pesticide residue, because cotton is one of the most heavily sprayed crops, and it's also one of the most genetically modified products. Studies show that the pesticides used on cotton lead to histamine release and other allergic reactions (Newball 1986).

Alternatives to chemically based clothing are those made from natural fibers such as certified-organic cotton, hemp, bamboo, and linen. Look for clothing colored with plant based dyes, which create more muted tones but are largely chemical-free. Any extra costs can be considered an investment in health, similar to buying organic foods. Choosing only organic fabrics with nontoxic colors for your undergarments, your exercise clothes (sweating releases the chemicals into your pores), and your children's clothing is especially recommended. You can find these items for affordable prices on etsy.com or with an Internet search.

Vintage clothing is even more affordable and often predates the chemical era or is old enough that the chemicals have dissipated.

As with anything, check labels of clothing. If it says "certified organic" and "fair trade labor," you're on your way. Just remember that clothing may be labeled "eco-friendly" but not necessarily be nontoxic if it's made from recycled polyester or other plastics.

These days, clothing is plentiful; cheap; and, sadly, disposable . . . but at a cost to our health and the health of clothing workers, who are exposed to these harsh chemicals, particularly in the inhumane sweatshops that are tragically all too common worldwide.

Bedding

Similar to chemicals on clothing, your bedding needs to be as nontoxic as possible. After all, you spend five or more hours a night lying on it.

Begin with your bed itself: if it is labeled as flame-retardant, then you are sleeping on a bed of toxic chemicals. True, it is important for safety reasons to avoid flammable materials. But what is the trade-off in terms of health concerns? Look for a certified-organic mattress made of pure rubber, available at specialty shops. These mattresses are comfortable and chemical-free.

At the very least, invest in certified-organic-fabric sheets, such as bamboo or cotton, which are conducive to sound sleep because the fabrics breathe. If comfort is a concern, choose bamboo, which is as soft as—or softer than—1,000-thread-count cotton.

Blankets and pillows should also be made from certified-organic fabrics with nontoxic dye colors. It's an investment in a good night's sleep, which helps you sparkle more brightly.

Air Pollutants

A good air purifier is also a worthwhile investment in your health. As you've read in this chapter, a lot of environmental toxins are inhaled as fumes. When you're out and about, do your best to avoid cigarette smoke, which has been shown to increase histamine levels, even when passively inhaled as secondhand smoke (Omini 1990).

Recent research also shows that *thirdhand* smoke (breathing cigarette smell on someone's clothing or spending time in a car where cigarettes have been smoked, for example) is carcinogenic (Sleiman 2010).

Electromagnetic Fields

As a highly sensitive person, you in all probability can feel the electromagnetic fields (EMFs) of electronics. Most likely, you have difficulty putting a cell phone to your ear and have to rely upon the phone's speaker. This is actually the healthiest choice!

Research has shown that exposure to electromagnetic fields stimulates our mast cells to release histamine, which leads to inflammation and other allergic reactions (Gangi 2000, Rajkovic 2005).

A study found that people who sit in front of televisions and computer monitors for as little as two hours have significant histamine release from their mast cells. Researchers said that EMFs can lead to "screen dermatitis" or skin allergies (Johansson 2001).

Your best bet is to invest in an EMF-detector device—which measures the electromagnetic fields of the electronics you use—available at hardware and online stores. There are also low-electromagnetic versions of most electronics these days, which are a valuable investment. Some companies sell electromagnetic shields.

Health practitioners advise unplugging electronics when not in use and keeping them away from you, especially while you're sleeping.

In the next chapter, we'll look at other natural ways to combat the stress response.

✳   ✳   ✳

CHAPTER EIGHT

Natural Stress, Depression, and Anxiety Relief

There's no doubt that medication helps alleviate symptoms of the trauma-drama cycle. However, as we've been discussing, the side effects of chemicals can be severe and can dull your sparkle. That's why *natural* remedies are so exciting.

Studies show that stress leads to histamine production, which in turn makes you wide-awake. Indeed, this is one of the reasons for the *addiction* to stress and drama—because of the stimulating effects of histamine and other neurotransmitters and hormones.

After a stressful day, then, you'll feel jittery and overly stimulated. That's when many people reach for sedative substances such as alcohol to relax or fall asleep. Trouble is, alcohol triggers further histamine production and disrupts REM sleep cycles. So alcohol does not yield a refreshing night's sleep, after all.

In this chapter, we'll look at flowers, herbs, and other natural remedies to promote rest and lower anxiety. When you get quality sleep, your brain can produce melatonin and convert it to serotonin—a process that helps you enjoy a good mood and naturally high energy. Serotonin also protects you from unhealthful food cravings.

I have personally tried and recommend each of the resources in this chapter. They are backed up by scientific literature, with studies showing that they are effective agents in healing the effects of trauma.

It may seem as if I'm giving you a lot of options in this chapter, so please look upon them as a "buffet" from which you can select what resonates with you. The more of these natural remedies you use, the better. Possible prescription-medicine interactions are noted for each description.

Some scientific studies show that these healing flowers, herbs, and lifestyle choices are just as powerful as—or even *more* powerful than—prescription medication in combatting depression and anxiety. They can also help you feel calm and sleep better.

Chamomile

Chamomile is a small daisy-like flower that, when dried and ingested, has a soothing and calming effect. It has been harvested medicinally since ancient times in Egyptian, Greek, and Roman cultures to treat respiratory, digestive, and skin issues.

Today, chamomile is most frequently used as a tea. Studies have found that the terpenoids and flavonoids in dried chamomile reduce anxiety and induce sleep. It's the perfect drink before bed.

A double-blind study of 61 people who had anxiety diagnoses showed that chamomile reduced their anxiety patterns significantly more than a placebo. Another study reported similar findings for depression (Amsterdam et al. 2009, 2012).

Chamomile is also anti-inflammatory. Many studies have found it to have beneficial health effects in warding off some cancers and heart disease. There's also evidence that breathing in steamed chamomile as a vapor can reduce common cold symptoms.

I drink a cup of chamomile tea first thing each morning, because I've learned that being relaxed is the best approach to a successful day. It's all about enjoying your work, not about going faster (by using caffeine or other stimulants).

Chamomile is so strong that it can interact with prescription drugs, so talk with your doctor and do research if you're currently on medication.

Saint-John's-wort

In addition to chamomile, another flower, *Hypericum perforatum,* is extracted for a remarkably healing compound called Saint-John's-wort.

A landmark study of 135 clinically depressed men and women compared the efficacy of Saint-John's-wort to that of Prozac. The study involved one-third of participants receiving Saint-John's-wort, one-third receiving Prozac, and one-third receiving a placebo. It was a double-blind study, so neither the researchers nor the patients were aware of who was receiving which treatment. At the end of 12 weeks, those who'd received Saint-John's-wort had the most significant decrease in their depressive symptoms (Fava et al. 2005). Saint-John's-wort beat out Prozac for helping with depression!

Another double-blind study of 1,200 depressed people treated with Saint-John's-wort came to a similar conclusion, noting that Saint-John's-wort extract "has a meaningful beneficial effect during acute treatment of patients suffering from mild depression and leads to a substantial increase in the probability of remission" (Kasper et al. 2008).

The more hyperforin (a component of Saint-John's-wort) that a dosage contains, the better it performs in reducing depression symptoms. One study found that dosages of 300 milligrams (mgs) with a hyperforin content of 5 percent performed best, while dosages with 0.5 percent hyperforin were comparable to the effects of a placebo (Laakmann et al. 1998).

Two drawbacks of Saint-John's-wort are that some people report dizziness or tiredness after taking the herb (fortunately, this is not a universal side effect) and that the flowers of Saint-John's-wort plants, which grow rapidly in the wild, are poisonous to some animals.

Lavender

The beautiful pale purple flower lavender has long been used as a relaxation and sleeping tool. Studies show that inhaling lavender significantly reduces anxiety and can help people with insomnia get to sleep.

Among these studies is one that found that inhaling lavender increased the percentage of the deep and light stages of sleep. The study concluded: "Lavender serves as a mild sedative" (Goel, Kim, and Lao 2005). Lavender inhalation before falling asleep also increased feelings of vigor in the morning.

A recent review of studies about the oral intake of lavender concluded that lavender supplements may have anxiolytic effects—that is, they provide stress and anxiety relief (Perry et al. 2012). One exciting study found that inhaling lavender decreased cortisol levels. Compared to drinking alcohol at night or taking sleeping pills, inhaling lavender is a way to fall asleep more easily and awaken without hangover effects.

It's helpful to spray lavender oil on your pillow and sheets each night. You can purchase this oil at health-food stores and online. Just make sure it's real lavender, not synthetic.

Citrus Essential Oils

Two major studies found that inhaling citrus essential oils (lemon, orange, or grapefruit) normalizes neuroendocrine hormone levels and immune function in depressed individuals significantly more than antidepressant medication. The researchers concluded that inhaling citrus essential oil "can restore the stress-induced immunosuppression, suggesting that citrus fragrance may have an effect on restoring the homeostatic balance" (Komori et al. 1995).

Melatonin

Melatonin, a hormone secreted at night by the pineal gland, helps you sleep well. If you maintain a healthful lifestyle, which includes receiving full-spectrum sunlight during the day, your brain will produce sufficient melatonin.

However, many people have lowered melatonin levels, especially as they age. A melatonin supplement is considered a safe and effective way to induce drowsiness and sleep. Most studies on melatonin show that people's moods are better the morning after taking it, because they've had a good night's rest. A double-blind study found that melatonin helped children to overcome their sleeping disorders without side effects (Jan, Espezel, and Appleton 1994).

There's some evidence that melatonin may also be anticarcinogenic, adding to its potential health benefits. You can purchase melatonin at most vitamin and supplement stores.

Valerian

The studies on the efficacy of valerian—an herb often used to induce sleep and reduce anxiety—have been mixed. Some show that valerian has the same effectiveness as a placebo, while others report significant benefits in combatting insomnia.

Valerian has a strong taste and aftertaste, so it's best to ingest it in a vegetarian capsule instead of directly drinking it. The good news is that valerian has few side effects, so it's a safe alternative to chemical sleeping agents.

Kava Kava

Kava kava, a plant grown on Pacific islands, has long been utilized as a sedative and intoxicant. It's available in liquid and pill form, from the root and leaves of the plant. Studies show that kava kava acts upon the dopamine receptors to bring about its euphoric effects.

Kava kava is illegal in some parts of the world, mostly because of concerns over its toxicity. However, manufacturers blame mold for the toxic reactions, and say that new tighter controls eliminate health hazards.

Several double-blind studies found that kava kava significantly reduced anxiety and depression levels, compared to a placebo. While a 2012 study found no adverse effects from kava kava, it does numb the mouth quite a bit, so if that's an unpleasant sensation to you, you may want to consider the capsule form.

Meditation Music

Soft, soothing music promotes relaxation, and studies are finding that having it on in the background reduces tension, negative emotions, and other effects of stress.

Here are some of the research findings:

— **Soft music provides healing help for post-traumatic stress reactions.** Several studies cite significant and measurable benefits derived from listening to soft music for those suffering from the effects of trauma, including alleviation of insomnia, promotion of better-quality sleep, and a reduction in overall symptoms.

— **Listening while you work is beneficial.** One study found that people completing a stressful task while listening to music didn't have an increase in cortisol levels, whereas study participants who engaged in the same stressful task in silence had significant cortisol increases.

— **The type of music makes a difference.** A comparison of people listening to either classical music, heavy-metal music, or no music found that classical music resulted in measurable calming effects . . . but silence and heavy metal did not. So, be discerning with regard to the music you listen to, as it affects your mood and energy.

— **Anxiety is reduced.** Studies show that anxiety levels and blood pressure are significantly lowered in those who listen to classical or meditation music prior to a stressful event (such as surgery).

— **Music is heart-healthy.** Cardiovascular patients showed so much improvement in heart rate while they listened to relaxing music, according to studies, that researchers recommended playing music bedside while people recover from heart surgery. The lead researcher concluded:

> The greatest benefit on health is visible with classical music and meditation music, whereas heavy metal music or techno are not only ineffective but possibly dangerous and can lead to stress and/or life-threatening arrhythmias. The music of many composers most effectively improves quality of life, will increase health and probably prolong life. (Trappe 2010)

— **Singing and listening are different.** An interesting study compared the cortisol and emotional levels in both choir singers and those who were listening to choir music. They found that singing increased cortisol levels but lowered negative emotions. Those who listened without singing experienced the opposite: their cortisol levels dropped, but their negative emotions increased. The increased cortisol levels in singers were probably due to performance anxiety because of the audience. Most likely those who sing alone would not show the same spike in the stress hormone.

From these studies, you can recognize the relaxation and health benefits of soft, meditative music. The more often you listen to soothing music, the better.

Fortunately, there are online radio stations that you can subscribe to and pay a small monthly fee to eliminate commercials (which can startle you out of your meditative state). YouTube also offers long meditation music videos for free. Use these search words to find soft online music: *meditation music, spa music, nature music,* and *relaxation music.*

Massage and Bodywork

Receiving a massage is a relaxing experience for most people, although some who are hypervigilant have difficulty dropping their guard during a body-treatment experience.

There's a difference between *massage* and *bodywork:*

✳ **Massage** is a process designed only for relaxation and to help you let go of tension.

✳ **Bodywork** is therapeutic (it's also known as "massage therapy") and is used to treat injuries, sore muscles, and emotional pain. Massage therapists and body-workers take extra classes to learn about physiology and specialized healing methods.

As I mentioned earlier, the women's psychiatric hospital unit that I directed had a bodyworker on staff. During her one-on-one sessions, patients would recover repressed memories, have helpful insights, and experience cathartic release of pent-up emotions.

Massage therapy lowers your cortisol levels and increases the levels of feel-good dopamine, oxytocin, and serotonin. So you feel relaxed and a sense of pleasure.

Studies overwhelmingly show that massage significantly reduces depression, anxiety, and post-traumatic symptoms; lowers blood pressure and heart rate; and improves sleep cycles.

Researchers studying traumatized National Guard veterans who had been deployed in Iraq reported that therapeutic massage resulted in "significant reductions in ratings of physical pain, physical tension, irritability, anxiety/worry, and depression after massage, and longitudinal analysis suggested declining baseline levels of tension and irritability" (Collinge, Kahn, and Soltysik 2012).

When choosing your massage therapist, look for someone who is experienced with trauma treatment. This therapist will understand if you experience strong emotions during the bodywork session. Experienced trauma massage therapists will remain neutral in conversations and keep their opinions to themselves to avoid inadvertently triggering the client.

Creating an Optimal Sleep Environment

You can fall asleep, and stay asleep, more easily with a few adjustments to your bedroom and nighttime habits:

- ✳ **Darken your bedroom.** Even a small nightlight will stimulate your brain and keep you from sleeping deeply.

- ✳ **Cool the room.** We sleep better in a bedroom with a cool air temperature. If you're cold, wear socks, which studies show leads to better sleep.

- ✳ **Avoid electronics.** Turn off your wireless Internet signal at night, and don't watch television or look at any electronic devices within an hour of your bedtime. Studies show that the "blue light" in technological gadgets (like tablets) disrupts circadian rhythms.

- ✳ **Go natural.** Natural cotton or bamboo sheets and blankets "breathe," so you avoid the night sweats from polyester bedding.

✳ **Exercise earlier**. Make sure your exercise schedule ends three hours before bedtime.

✳ **Keep the bedroom relaxing**. Don't do work in bed to ensure that the bedroom is associated only with relaxation.

Gratitude

Several experiments have studied the relationship between gratitude and well-being. Some participants wrote daily journal entries about what they were grateful for, and others wrote about difficulties and struggles. The gratitude-journal groups showed significantly higher levels of well-being in all of the studies, including one that focused on veterans who exhibited post-traumatic stress traits (Kashdan, Uswatte, and Julian 2006).

Based upon this research, it's a good idea to count your blessings daily. Keeping a gratitude journal (either in book-diary form or on the computer) serves as a reminder to view the glass as half-full, instead of half-empty.

Spirituality, Religion, and Prayer

Much research has verified that having a spiritual or religious practice increases well-being. This is not to say that you must be religious or spiritual to be happy—just that those who do have a belief system *are,* on average, happier.

I know that my own healing from post-traumatic symptoms is largely because of my strong faith in God, Jesus, Holy Spirit, and my guardian angels. Whenever I felt anxious, prayer would calm me.

By consistently attending a church, temple, or spiritual gathering, you develop a loving support group of people who will be there for you physically and emotionally. Furthermore, several studies found that the more involved someone is in his or her spirituality or religious practices, the less likely he or she is to abuse drugs.

Having a spiritual or religious practice reduces the severity of post-traumatic symptoms, according to research. A major study conducted upon 532 U.S. veterans in a PTSD treatment program found: "Specifically, veterans who scored higher on adaptive dimensions of spirituality (daily spiritual experiences, forgiveness, spiritual practices, positive religious coping, and organizational religiousness) at intake fared significantly better in this program" (Currier, Holland, and Drescher 2015).

Positive religious coping means that you have a faith-based belief that the trauma had existential meaning, rather than being a random event. Those who exhibit positive religious coping are more likely to seek support from their spiritual or religious community.

Several studies have concluded that people who hold beliefs about a punishing God are more likely to develop post-traumatic symptoms. Those who believe God caused or allowed the trauma to happen were found to have more post-traumatic symptoms. This is attributable to their lacking a sense of control over future crises, since they believe that events are up to the whim of God, who may choose to punish them at any time.

For those who believe in a compassionate God, though, most researchers refer to the "protective effect" of spirituality and religion, because these factors seem to safeguard believers from depression, substance abuse, and other post-traumatic symptoms.

Breathing-Based Meditation

Most of us are familiar with the general concept of meditation, as it has been cited in the popular press for decades. Like *yoga,* the word *meditation* can appear intimidating, as if it's reserved for those who practice alternative lifestyles. Meditation can seem irrelevant and airy-fairy until you read the scientific literature supporting its healing effects.

Many studies have been conducted upon war veterans who have post-traumatic symptoms. Measuring the effects of meditation courses on veterans, researchers have shown that "breathing-based meditation" methods lead to significant reduction of hypervigilance and anxiety for those who've been traumatized.

Diaphragmatic breathing (also known as "belly breathing") is a conscious way of breathing deeply and rhythmically. You inhale a full breath so that your rib cage and belly expand. Putting your hand on your stomach helps you monitor that you are in fact doing belly breathing instead of shallow breathing. With belly breathing, you inhale a larger amount of oxygen.

Studies of belly breathing show promising results, with these demonstrated benefits:

※ Increased oxygen to cells

※ Decreased carbon dioxide and other waste products

※ Parasympathetic nervous-system activation (calming)

※ Reduced anxiety

※ Increased confidence

※ Lowered heart rate and blood pressure

The more you practice belly breathing, the more calming benefits you receive. This is a practice that you can do *anywhere,* including during stressful situations at work.

Another form of meditation called *mindfulness* also holds promise for reducing post-traumatic symptoms. A Harvard University study discovered that mindfulness meditation decreased activation and volume of gray matter of the amygdala, a region of the brain involved in fear processing (Hölzel et al. 2010).

According to research, meditation can heal the brain and make positive physiological changes to the brain's structure, processing routines, and chemistry.

Other Calming Experiences

Of course, there are many other ways to calm the mind and body, such as creative arts and spending time in nature. As you are guided, you are the best judge of what calms and soothes you.

A calming mode of exercise—yoga—is the subject of the next chapter.

CHAPTER NINE

Gentle and Restorative Yoga

There are two categories of coping after a trauma: *avoidant coping* and *active coping.*

As I touched on previously, avoidant coping means you avoid facing painful memories by minimizing the impact they had upon you, through emotional numbing, isolating yourself, and dissociating.

Active coping, in contrast, means that you deal directly with healing the trauma and your underlying feelings about yourself and about life. This usually involves going to trauma-focused talk therapy (psychotherapy) with a qualified therapist who knows how to deal with post-trauma symptoms. If you have many choices for a therapist, then go with one who specializes in trauma recovery. (We will discuss therapeutic options further in Chapter 10.)

Studies also show that being *active* in terms of exercising your body is helpful in healing the symptoms. Exercise is cathartic and can build self-confidence. Just be sure that the workout program you choose isn't in itself stressful, as that will increase your cortisol, adrenaline, and histamine levels.

✳ *Active-cognitive coping* means meditating, or changing your mind about how you view life so that it's more positive.

✳ *Active-behavioral coping* means dealing with emotional pain through activities, including exercise like yoga.

Gentle and restorative yoga provides a wonderful healing outlet for trauma survivors. Yoga is the exercise program most often recommended to heal post-traumatic symptoms and to reduce stress hormones and the experience of stress.

If the idea of yoga classes conjures visions of you standing in a room full of skinny, flexible 20-year-olds . . . well, there's a reason for that. As you'll read in this chapter, yoga is an amazing weight-loss and youth-enhancing tool.

However, studies show that you don't have to pound it out with frantic sun salutations and fast-paced warrior poses in order to gain benefits from yoga. In fact, as you'll read, *gentle* and *restorative* yoga is proving beneficial in healing the mind and body.

Besides, there's a lot of evidence that doing stressful exercise—including yoga—is counterproductive. Stressful exercise is competitive or brings up fear and triggers the adrenal glands to produce the stress hormone cortisol. This, in turn, causes the body to store food as fat, particularly in the stomach. Stress makes the brain and body think that you are in danger, and that famine is on the way. So, it holds on to every calorie as self-protection.

This part of the puzzle was revolutionary to me. I'd exercise daily, and couldn't understand why I wasn't losing weight. Well, it was because my exercise program was too stressful and was triggering cortisol production.

Gentle exercise is actually a better method for weight loss, because little or no cortisol is produced. So your body becomes more "fuel-efficient" in terms of burning off the food you eat.

I once read an article in a women's magazine called "Apply Your Makeup to Achieve That Just-Got-Out-of-Yoga-Class Glow." I laughed, because the article *so* misses the point of yoga. The reason why yoga gives a natural, not-made-up glow is because this ancient form of stretching circulates oxygen and blood within your body.

Apart from the aesthetic benefits of yoga is its remarkable ability to heal the effects of stress and trauma.

Stress Management and Yoga

An impressive 2011 study followed 30 female college students who took daily 35-minute yoga classes for 12 weeks. These students were matched for age, height, and weight with a "control group" of female students who did not participate in yoga.

During college examination time, both the yoga and control groups had their stress levels measured for comparison. Heart rate, blood pressure, respiratory rates, anxiety levels, and serum cortisol levels were tested, as a measure of how the students were handling the stress of test taking.

The results were significant: Both groups had comparable cortisol levels at the beginning of the study. But after three months of daily yoga, the yoga group's cortisol levels during examination time were markedly lower than the control group's. In addition, the yoga group exhibited statistically significant lower heart and respiratory rates, blood pressure, and anxiety, compared to the control group (Gopal et al. 2011).

Studies such as this one point to the way that yoga teaches us a different approach to stress.

Yoga Reduces Premenstrual Syndrome Symptoms

A study of women suffering from premenstrual syndrome (PMS) symptoms were divided into two groups: one who took daily 40-minute yoga classes, and another group who didn't do yoga. After three months of the classes, the difference in PMS symptoms was significant (Kanojia et al. 2013).

The yoga group displayed a significant decrease in premenstrual anger, depression, and anxiety. They also reported an increase in feelings of well-being, directly attributable to their new yoga practice.

Yoga is one of the most highly recommended methods for healing post-traumatic symptoms. You'll notice that in this study and that of the college students, and in many other yoga studies, the great results didn't require 90-minute yoga classes. These two studies were based upon 35- to 40-minute classes! Healing benefits from yoga can be attained in as little as 35 minutes per class, provided that you practice regularly.

> YOGA IS ONE OF THE MOST HIGHLY RECOMMENDED METHODS FOR HEALING POST-TRAUMATIC SYMPTOMS. HEALING BENEFITS FROM YOGA CAN BE ATTAINED IN AS LITTLE AS 35 MINUTES PER CLASS, PROVIDED THAT YOU PRACTICE REGULARLY.

Yoga Heals Effects of Trauma

The freeze response is a natural adaptation to dangerous situations, allowing us the ability to assess whether to run or fight. When we feel completely trapped with no escape, though, our body shuts down and we go into a state of temporary paralysis, or "freeze." Stress hormones like adrenaline and cortisol flood the body and brain as we prepare ourselves for action.

Normally, the freeze response is followed by the body shaking uncontrollably as a way of discharging stress hormones. However, some people remain in a frozen state, and the stress hormones and horror of the trauma are retained.

The freeze response can stay in the body long after the traumatic situation is removed. The person's muscles are then stiff and tense, which can lead to soreness and illness.

The freeze response is holding the emotions of the traumatic moments, and it needs to be peacefully released, usually through catharsis such as body movement like yoga. Those who hold on to their fear can become detached from their bodily sensations, and feel like they are constantly out of their body in a dissociative state. They may also develop "flat affect," meaning that they don't feel or show strong positive or negative emotions. In addition, their muscles and body may be stiff and uptight, including having constipation.

Studies show that yoga heals stored trauma because it . . .

✷ . . . brings your focus back into your body.

✷ . . . grounds you in a peaceful, pleasant way.

✷ . . . restores the sense that it's safe to return your consciousness to your body, and be aware of here-and-now bodily sensations.

✳ . . . reduces spaciness and dissociation.

✳. . . reduces hypervigilance, and allows you to feel safe.

One of the measures of whether trauma has changed your physiology is called *heart rate variability* (HRV). In those who've been affected by trauma, the brain's arousal system is set on hypervigilance. You're constantly on alert for danger, as a way of controlling or avoiding it.

Those unaffected by trauma have a strong HRV, in which their nervous system rests appropriately. Small stressors are no big deal to them.

In contrast, traumatized individuals have a lower HRV, which means they "overreact" to small stressors as if they were a crisis. Even though the trauma was in the past, their brains treat new stimuli as if they're new traumas.

Bessel van der Kolk, M.D., the founder and medical director of the Trauma Center at Justice Resource Institute, discovered that yoga corrects our HRV. This means that we aren't upset by life's "little things" as much. Yoga literally resets the brain wiring to keep us calmer. Since a low HRV from trauma is associated with the development of serious illness, this research about yoga restoring normal HRV is significant.

Yoga helps the hypothalamus of trauma survivors to restore its ability to react to stress in healthy ways, instead of overreacting as if everything were a dangerous emergency. There's also evidence that the parasympathetic nervous system (which is associated with relaxation and calm) is strengthened with yoga practice.

Yoga also decreases the flow of the stress hormone cortisol, as well as reducing anxiety and resting heart rate. One review of scientific studies about yoga concluded: "Yogic practices inhibit the areas responsible for fear, aggressiveness, and rage, and stimulate the rewarding centers in the median forebrain and other areas, leading to a state of bliss and pleasure" (Woodyard 2011).

Weight Loss and Yoga

Yoga is great for weight loss! A recent review of studies on the connection between yoga and weight loss concluded that yoga provides "successful intervention for weight maintenance, prevention of obesity, and risk reduction for diseases in which obesity plays a significant causal role" (Rioux and Ritenbaugh 2013).

A Seattle study of 15,550 adults ages 53 to 57 found that among participants of normal weight, those who practiced yoga for four years gained significantly less weight than those who didn't practice yoga (9.5 pounds versus 12.6 pounds). Moreover, overweight participants in the yoga group *lost* an average of 5 pounds, whereas those who were overweight in the non-yoga group gained an average of 18.5 pounds (Kristal et al. 2005).

Not surprisingly, researchers say that weight loss increases the more often you do yoga, and also if you have a home-based yoga practice.

How Yoga Reduces Weight

✳ Yoga relieves stress, which reduces your likelihood of binge-eating foods for stress reduction.

✳ Yoga lowers cortisol levels, which can reduce the stored fat in your stomach area.

✳ People who regularly practice yoga are calmer and actually rewire their brains to stay away from stress, according to research conducted by the National Center for Complementary and Alternative Medicine.

✳ Yoga improves sleep quality.

✳ Yoga makes you more mindful of what you eat, which leads to portion control and healthier food choices.

✳ Yoga increases insulin sensitivity, which signals the body to use food for energy, instead of storing it as fat.

Yoga Reduces Back Pain

Yoga also reduces back pain, improves flexibility, and can lower blood pressure, according to scientific research. Dr. James Raub, a scientist with the National Center for Environmental Assessment who studies yoga's health benefits, wrote:

> There is a need to have yoga better recognized by the health care community as a complement to conventional medical care. Over the last 10 years, a growing number of research studies have shown that the practice of Hatha Yoga can improve strength and flexibility, and may help control such physiological variables as blood pressure, respiration and heart rate, and metabolic rate to improve overall exercise capacity. (Raub 2002)

A 2011 study of 313 adults with chronic or recurring low-back pain concluded that three months of weekly yoga classes resulted in better function than traditional medical care (Tilbrook et al. 2011).

A six-month study of 135 seniors ages 65 to 85 reported on the outcome of those who practiced yoga, versus those who did no exercise and those who did conventional exercise (walking, jogging, and the like). The conclusion of the study was: "Those in the yoga group showed significant improvement in quality-of-life and physical measures compared to exercise and wait-list control groups" (Oken et al. 2006).

Light Yin and Yang Yoga

Regaining your sparkle means choosing the brightest path possible in whatever you do. That includes yoga.

Not all yoga classes are the same. Some are very yang (masculine energy) because they focus upon building strong core muscles, raising the heart rate, and moving fast. These classes commonly have a lot of warrior *asanas* (poses), which are very yang.

If you have a stressful lifestyle, you're overloaded with yang energy in your life—especially *dark* yang, with its emphasis on competition and winning; the last thing you need is to add more of this to your life by taking a yoga class that focuses on comparing yourself to others, or competing with your classmates.

Other classes are more yin (feminine energy), with a focus upon stretching, restoration, breathing, centering, balance, and inner peace. These classes tend to have more mat work, as opposed to standing work. The teacher generally speaks in a soft, meditative voice, with soothing music in the background. While doing lying-down mat poses, you're encouraged to keep your eyes closed and focus upon your inner experience of yoga.

Dark yin energy occurs in yoga classes when you feel jealous of other students, feel bad about your body or skill level, and worry that the yoga instructor will shame you with a public pose correction.

If you're feeling stressed, avoid crowded yoga studios. Studies show that feeling crowded brings up aggressive and competitive tendencies—definitely dark yang energies.

Instead, choose a yoga class that has bright yin and yang energies. These are love based rather than fear based.

Dark Yin and Yang Yoga-Class Characteristics	Bright Yin and Yang Yoga-Class Characteristics
Crowdedness	Spaciousness
Competitiveness	Cooperation
Loud music and instruction	Gentle music and instruction
Fast pace	Flowing pace
Strenuous feeling	Good feeling
Painful muscles	Refreshed muscles
Irritability after class	Peacefulness after class
Lack of community with other students	Community feeling with other students

In a bright yin and yang yoga class, you feel safe, nurtured, and supported. When the instructor guides you, you feel glad to receive the guidance (instead of shamed, as occurs in the dark yang and yin yoga classes).

Even though the bright-energy yoga classes are usually labeled "restorative," "yin," or "gentle" yoga, you'll want to research that the instructor of the class really does teach with gentle energy.

Some yoga classes advertised as "gentle" or "restorative" are actually very dark yang or yin. This usually happens when instructors who are accustomed to teaching level 2, challenging classes substitute for a gentler class. So inquire about the teacher ahead of time.

Restorative Yoga

Yoga classes labeled as "restorative" usually have a soft and gentle "light yin" feel to them. Many of the poses are conducted while lying down, using bolsters, blankets, blocks, straps, and walls to stretch your muscles in pleasant ways. The poses are held for up to 15 minutes at a time, which allows the muscles to let go of tension.

Restorative yoga classes are supportive of people's physical differences, and they don't have a sense of competition or perfectionism that you find in some yoga classes. They don't tend to attract the more experienced students, so there's less chance of unfavorable comparison of yourself to others. The teacher of one of my favorite restorative classes uses brass Tibetan bowls to make soothing sounds during class. The whole energy of restorative yoga is meditative.

Restorative classes are slower paced, but they still provide benefits. Restorative yoga even leads to weight loss!

In a recent study, a group of mature overweight women (average age of 55) was divided into two subgroups: one taking restorative yoga and the other practicing stretching exercises without a yoga component. At the end of 48 weeks, the yoga group had lost 34 square centimeters of subcutaneous fat, while the stretch group had only lost 6.6 square centimeters. The yoga group also lost significantly more weight compared to the stretch group. The researchers concluded that the difference was the reduced cortisol production in the yoga group (Araneta et al. 2013). As you'll recall, cortisol is involved in the storing of belly fat and an increased appetite.

Yoga instructors often say that strong emotions are stored in our hips. They say that doing hip-opening yoga poses, such as pigeon or stretching open your legs, will release stored emotions. In restorative yoga classes, where you're holding hip-opening poses for long periods of time, you can receive helpful insights that allow you to integrate your past.

Home-Based Yoga

Let's be real: it's time-consuming to drive to a yoga studio, take a 90-minute class, and then drive back home. Plus, if it's a crowded studio, you have to arrive at class ahead of time in order to find a good spot on the floor! So, we're talking about two to three hours.

An alternative is to do yoga at home, or at a nearby friend's home. If your budget permits, you can call any yoga studio and hire a personal instructor. The going rate for a home visit is between US$50 and $100. This sounds expensive compared to the average $15 price of taking a studio class. However, if you don't go to yoga classes at studios because of time constraints, it doesn't matter what they cost.

If you have some friends who are interested in doing yoga, you can split the cost with them . . . plus enjoy a fun and healthy experience with your buddies!

An instructor who comes to your home can give you guidance about your poses to ensure you're being safe. You actually get much more attention than in a crowded yoga class, plus you lose the fear of being embarrassed in front of the other students. Once your body gets the memory of how to safely do the basic yoga poses, then you may be able to do yoga on your own.

YouTube is filled with wonderful free yoga-class videos, and many of them are labeled "gentle," "yin," and "restorative." The instructors will give you tips on how to safely practice each pose.

A Note about Yoga for Christians

Some Christians are wary of the Eastern religious bases of the yoga tradition, with concerns about opening themselves up to unknown energies. If this is your belief, then you could substitute an exercise such as Pilates, which will have the same positive results.

You might also consider Christian-based yoga programs. These practices combine yoga poses with the chanting of Biblical verses. To find these, simply conduct an Internet search of the terms "Holy Yoga," "Scripture Yoga," or "Yoga Faith."

✳ ✳ ✳

Studies show (and you probably already know from experience) that when you're stressed, your muscles become tight with tension. So, yoga is a wonderful active coping strategy to stretch your muscles, heal effects of trauma, and release stress.

Another form of active coping is seeking outside support, as we will discuss in the next chapter.

CHAPTER TEN

Getting Support

Having support for changing your lifestyle is highly recommended. Making major changes brings up strong emotions, inner battles with your ego, and resistance to being told what to do. In this chapter, we'll look at the support options that are backed by scientific research.

Hundreds of studies have been conducted with those who have post-traumatic stress symptoms, trying to assess which methods are most helpful to them. The agreement among researchers is that cognitive-behavioral therapy (CBT) and eye movement desensitization and reprocessing (EMDR) are the two most effective clinical procedures for healing symptoms of trauma.

CBT

Here is an explanation of the scope of *cognitive-behavioral therapy,* outlined in a review of all the studies on healing methods for post-traumatic stress symptoms:

Cognitive-behavioral psychotherapy encompasses a myri-
ad of approaches (i.e. systematic desensitization, relaxation
training, biofeedback, cognitive processing therapy, stress inoculation training, assertiveness training, exposure therapy,
combined stress inoculation training and exposure therapy,
combined exposure therapy and relaxation training and cognitive therapy). (Iribarren et al. 2005)

The review of treatment options concluded that trauma-
focused cognitive-behavioral therapy was successful for treating post-traumatic stress symptoms that include borderline
personality disorder or substance abuse.

There are many forms of psychotherapy other than
cognitive behavioral, but there aren't enough studies supporting their efficacy in terms of healing from the effects
of trauma. Finding a therapist who specializes in healing
trauma helps ensure that you're working with someone who
is experienced and who understands the multiple layers of
trauma recovery.

The research shows that post-traumatic stress symptoms
are reduced when exposure therapy is included with cognitive-behavioral therapy. *Exposure therapy* refers to the process
whereby you literally face your fears. In most cases, the therapist will guide you to visualize or "feel" the scene of your
trauma. This is done gently, with lots of breaks so that you can
process your feelings with the therapist. This is different from
catharsis, which trauma pioneer Peter Levine has found to be
ineffective at lessening trauma symptoms.

When I went through exposure therapy, I was guided to
imagine the traumatic scene appearing on a television set.
Then the image became full of static, and finally disappeared
from the screen. This single process greatly reduced the emotional impact of the traumatic image, allowing me to deal with

it on an even deeper level, and connecting it to childhood events I'd repressed. Exposure therapy sounds intense, and it is . . . but it's worth it.

EMDR

Eye movement desensitization and reprocessing was developed in 1987 by Francine Shapiro. The idea came to Francine after she realized that she felt emotional relief if her eyes were moving when she remembered an upsetting situation. Francine developed research on eye movements to help people with post-traumatic symptoms.

EMDR may be related to rapid eye movement (REM), which occurs during dream time. While we are dreaming, our unconscious mind is processing the day's events.

EMDR's effectiveness in reducing post-traumatic symptoms has been widely studied and validated. Most studies show that EMDR reduces symptoms and has lasting results.

EMDR is a very emotionally involved process that triggers old memories of situations reminding you of the trauma. Strong emotions are brought to the surface in a safe and contained setting with an experienced therapist. Once the emotions surface, they lose their hidden grip on you. I found EMDR to be very intense, but also extremely healing and freeing.

The process of EMDR begins with a clinical interview of your life history, focusing on your traumatic experiences and post-traumatic symptoms. Subsequent sessions utilize equipment such as headphones with pulsating sounds that alternate between your ears, or alternating-pulsing handheld devices. EMDR may also involve the therapist using two fingers to direct your eyes back and forth.

It's important to only work with therapists who have received training in how to conduct EMDR, a list of whom you can find at emdr.com.

There are also free EMDR meditations available on You Tube, which may be soothing but have not been clinically tested for effectiveness.

Support Groups for Emotional and Mental Health

Online and in-person support groups for those with post-traumatic symptoms are available, many of them free or low-cost. In these group settings, you'll meet with other people who have experienced debilitating trauma. It's a relief to discover that you're not alone in your feelings, behaviors, and symptoms. Group therapy and support groups help you to accept yourself, because you can see how likable other people similar to you are.

Typing "PTSD support group" in your Internet search engine will help you find one. Some are free of charge, some accept health insurance if a licensed professional facilitates the group, and some charge money.

The 12-step model developed to help alcoholics (Alcoholics Anonymous) is also used in support groups for emotional and familial issues, both in person in most cities internationally and online. You can find a local or online 12-step group in your area with an Internet search for "12-step" and then the name of addiction from which you want to recover.

Twelve-step groups are free of charge, but do ask for donations. You can enlist the help of a sponsor—a person who's been in the program for a year or more—whom you call daily as you work on your 12 steps (a series of behaviors that help to free you from addictions).

Each 12-step meeting has its own "personality," based upon the regulars who attend. Try out various groups to find one where you feel the most comfortable.

EMOTIONAL SUPPORT

Emotions Anonymous is the 12-step group for emotional issues including post-traumatic symptoms, phobias, and psychological diagnoses. When I was a psychotherapist, I had clients who attended this group with great success.

FAMILY SUPPORT

If your birth or by-marriage family issues trigger anxiety, fear, guilt, or shame in you, these 12-step support groups are helpful and healing:

❋ **Adult Children of Alcoholics (ACA):** Healing help, support, and education for those who grew up in alcoholic homes.

❋ **Al-Anon:** Support and education for those who love an alcoholic or addict.

❋ **Alateen:** For adolescents with alcoholic family members.

❋ **Co-Dependents Anonymous:** For those seeking to heal from, and receive education about, co-dependency issues.

Support for Healing Addictions

Addictions are a major post-trauma symptom, as the person seeks to numb fears and other emotional pain. Yet, addictions are also the source of additional painful trauma and drama. There are healthier and more effective ways to deal with emotional pain. That's why 12-step groups can lead to a happier and more productive life. There are 12-step groups for most addictions. Here are examples of the groups that are available to help you:

✳ **Alcoholics Anonymous**—to receive support in abstaining from alcohol consumption.

✳ **Debtors Anonymous**—to overcome compulsive spending.

✳ **Gamblers Anonymous**—to receive support to stop gambling.

✳ **Narcotics Anonymous**—to recover from the addiction to prescription and illicit drugs.

✳ **Sex and Love Addicts Anonymous**—to stop the cycle of toxic and addictive relationships.

Support for Dietary Changes

The one addiction that you can't completely abstain from is food. So support can help you in developing a healthy relationship with it. The group **Overeaters Anonymous** offers meetings free of charge, but donations are gratefully accepted.

A 1991 Gallup poll of 1,000 Overeaters Anonymous members and a 2001 survey of 231 members both reached the same conclusion: the more someone commits to attending Overeaters Anonymous meetings, contacting his or her sponsor, and following the food plan (usually this means abstaining from a "binge food"—one that triggers anxiety and binge eating), the greater his or her success.

You can find an Overeaters Anonymous meeting near to you, or an online meeting, through an Internet search.

✳ ✳ ✳

I've attended support groups both personally and professionally, and I can attest that they do provide unique help. You can meet like-minded, compassionate people who understand you and who genuinely want to see you feel better. After you spend time in the group, you can become a sponsor to help newcomers. This is called "fellowship," and it's a valuable benefit of joining together in group support.

In Part III, we'll discuss how you can cultivate fellowship and mutual support in all your relationships . . . and make them sparkle!

PART III

Sparkling Around

Other People

INTRODUCTION TO PART III

Connecting with Others

Your relationships with other people can affect your happiness, health, finances, post-traumatic symptomatology— and your sparkle. While it's easy to fantasize about being all alone where no one can bother you, the truth is that we do have a need for human companionship. In Part III, we'll explore what healthy relationships look like and how to find them.

When you think about making new friends, you might:

✳ Wonder *where* you can find friendship

✳ Struggle with unworthiness, and worry whether other people would want to be friends with you

✳ Be concerned about finding quality friends who are genuine and trustworthy

If your past history with other people has been challenging, you may be wary of trying again. That's probably because your previous relationships had dysfunctional elements that made them more painful than pleasurable. Being traumatized, especially in childhood, makes it difficult to trust people.

With a history of trauma and a subsequent addiction to stress and drama, it's challenging to choose friends and partners healthfully. Most likely, you have been attracted to high-drama people. Or, trauma has triggered feelings of unworthiness, so you haven't attempted to connect with people you admire and respect.

Yet we all have a psychological need for *affiliation*, which means having emotional and physical connections with like-minded people.

Having friendships is correlated with better health and also with reduced cortisol levels when you're in stressful situations. Knowing that you've got good people in your corner who love and understand you—whether they are your friends, a romantic partner, or family—insulates you from stress hormones.

CHAPTER ELEVEN

How Do You Feel about Other People?

If you've been traumatized, you may have difficulties being around other people. Researchers have found that isolation and avoidance are two coping methods among those who've experienced trauma.

You may feel shy or not good enough. Perhaps you've endured painful rejection, and you avoid people to ensure this doesn't happen again.

The experience of trauma may have opened new levels of spirituality and philosophical understanding within you. So engaging in social exchanges may feel superficial and like a waste of time.

You may not know how to have conversations. Studies show that those who develop an *avoidant personality* are constantly monitoring themselves and others' reactions during dialogues. This leads to the avoidant person having an awkward, self-conscious style of speaking. This awkwardness can lead to further social rejection and subsequent phobias of being embarrassed and feeling inadequate around other people.

The avoidant personality is defined as a person who extremely limits interactions with other people in business or personal settings because of a preoccupying belief that there's something wrong with him or her that others would reject. Such an individual avoids people to shield him- or herself from social pain.

Examples include:

✳ Choosing a job where you can avoid personal interactions

✳ Avoiding social settings such as events, parties, and celebrations

✳ Only getting involved with another person if there's a reassurance you won't be rejected

✳ Being convinced that others are constantly criticizing or rejecting you, and having a hypersensitivity to criticism

✳ Choosing friends and romantic partners who are much lower on socioeconomic scales than you because they seem "safer" than someone at your own level

✳ Being preoccupied with your own perceived inadequacies

✳ Being self-conscious with other people, to the point where normal conversations are difficult

Social phobias and avoidant personality disorder have similar symptoms; however, the symptoms are much stronger and more debilitating in someone who has an avoidant personality. Cognitive therapy can be effective in treating this disorder so that the person can learn how to enjoy and trust other people's companionship.

Attachment

"Attachment issues" are part of the spectrum of trauma. If you were neglected, ridiculed, or in other ways abused as a child, you then develop difficulties with relationships. This includes:

✳ **Distrust.** If your basic parent-child trust was betrayed, it's difficult to trust anyone ever again.

✳ **Lack of boundaries.** It's difficult for you to know where you end and someone else begins. To practice boundaries, you have to be aware of how you feel . . . which is something that's outside the awareness of many childhood-trauma survivors. Cognitive therapy will give you insights about "enmeshment issues," in which you and your parent overly identified with each other, and you may have unconsciously absorbed your parent's fears.

✳ **Isolation.** It feels safer to be by yourself, even if it's lonely.

✳ **Detachment.** You're not aware of how other people feel and miss their nonverbal cues that would tell you so.

Attachment issues can be healed through developing at least one healthy and dependable relationship (which could be with your therapist). The methods for healing from trauma that you read about in Part II of this book can relieve the anxiety basis of attachment issues. Mostly, healing involves understanding the basis for these issues and then learning new ways to connect with others.

Isolating, Retreating, or Loneliness?

If you relate to the concept of an avoidant personality, you've got a lot of company. Those who've experienced trauma tend to isolate themselves because of their increased sensitivity, hypervigilance, and desire to protect against experiencing trauma again.

If you recognize these traits in yourself, it's important to tread carefully. There's a big need to balance your alone time without isolating yourself.

On the one hand, studies show that having "strategic retreats," where you spend a moderate amount of time alone, has a positive effect in relieving depressive symptoms. Researchers call this *constructive solitude,* where you have time to think, plan, and rest.

In contrast, *destructive solitude* is isolation without positive growth. An example is isolating yourself with mood-numbing chemicals or junk food, pushing others away with anger, and refusing offers of help.

However, some people have a higher need for affiliation—that is, social connection—than others. Here are characteristics of those with high affiliation needs:

✳ Desire to belong to a group

✳ Urge to be liked and tendency to go along with whatever the rest of the group wants to do

✳ A preference for collaboration, instead of competition

✳ Dislike of risk or uncertainty

If you have a high need for affiliation but stay isolated because you're afraid of rejection or haven't met the "right people" yet, then you're likely feeling lonely.

THE HIGH PRICE OF LONELINESS

Research shows that loneliness is harmful to us physically and emotionally. For one thing, it can drive a person to use mood-numbing drugs and alcohol. One study concluded: "The feeling of loneliness is stronger in drug abusers rather than non-drug [abusers, who] could develop the sense of being different from community and increase the probability of taking high risk behaviors and abusing drugs" (Hosseinbor et al. 2014). Another study of veterans with post-traumatic symptoms found that those who exhibited high levels of avoidant coping behavior were twice as likely to abuse alcohol.

Many researchers believe that avoidant personality is based upon the trauma of having one or more parents reject you. The feeling of being rejected is subjective—that is, it's up to the individual's interpretation whether a parent's behavior is rejecting or not. If you perceive yourself as being rejected by a parent, this experience creates a hunger for love and acceptance, with a simultaneous belief that you're not worthy of either.

Rejection in any form is stressful, even when it's in a movie you're watching. In one study of the effects of affiliation and rejection on stress, researchers had participants watch three different movie clips: one showing social rejection, one showing social acceptance, and one showing a socially neutral scene. After watching each movie clip, participants had their hormones measured. The social-rejection movie clip significantly raised cortisol levels in participants, once again demonstrating that your body reacts to social stress whether it's happening to you or on the screen (Wirth and Schultheiss 2006).

> STUDIES SHOW THAT YOUR BODY REACTS TO SOCIAL STRESS, WHETHER IT'S HAPPENING TO YOU OR TO AN ACTOR ON THE MOVIE SCREEN.

If you turn to mood-numbing substances to deal with social-rejection pain, chances are high that you'll become involved with other substance abusers. When someone is chronically high or drunk, they have no love to give. Their hearts are chemically closed. So you may be "with" someone and still not get your needs for love met.

Not only is loneliness emotionally painful, but it's physically painful, too. One study followed 220 people with fibromyalgia in which participants made entries in an electronic diary four times a day for 21 days. The researchers reported: "On mornings when individuals experienced higher than their usual levels of loneliness, they experienced higher levels of afternoon maladaptive pain cognitions, which in turn predicted increases in evening pain above the level of morning pain." They concluded: "Lonely episodes are associated with subsequent increases in negative patterns of thinking about pain, which in turn predict subsequent increases in bodily pain within a day" (Wolf et al. 2015).

Similarly, another study of 176 women with fibromyalgia found: "Positive social engagement offers relief from [fibromyalgia] fatigue that carries over across days and may provide an additional target to enhance the effectiveness of current interventions" (Yeung 2014).

You can be with people and still be lonely, if you don't feel understood, accepted, and heard within the relationship. Or if you have a high need to be with others yet don't know how to choose an appropriate friend or romantic partner, you'll be setting yourself up for more drama and stress through a dysfunctional relationship. Don't worry, though, as there are many suggestions for choosing healthier partners in the next chapter, where we will discuss interpersonal relationships.

The Oxytocin Connection

Trauma and stress play a biological role in loneliness, avoidant personality, and social phobias. As you'll recall from earlier in the book, those who have been traumatized are statistically more likely to encounter future trauma and stress.

All of this stress creates a flood of cortisol because the body feels threatened. One of the negative side effects of excess cortisol is that it reduces production of oxytocin, the hormone involved in fostering emotional intimacy in relationships.

You may have heard of oxytocin in discussions about sexual arousal. But recent findings show that it is an emotionally healing chemical as well, especially with respect to relationship interactions. Having sufficient oxytocin helps with learning how to trust and connect with others. The hormone also lowers anxiety.

Oxytocin is released from the pituitary gland in response to touch, such as hugging or getting a massage. It's not limited to human contact, either: oxytocin is released when you stroke your pet animal, too.

Scientists consider oxytocin to be essential for bonding with someone else. So touching, holding, being massaged, and being held can help heal avoidant and isolation tendencies.

You can purchase oxytocin inhalers; however, assuming they contain pure ingredients, oxytocin only has a "life span" of three minutes. So any benefits of inhaling a spray would be short-lived.

One way to overcome loneliness and increase your oxytocin levels is to adopt a pet. Another is to ask your trusted friends for hugs, since hugging increases oxytocin levels.

Humans' Best Friend

Let me begin this section by saying that I love *all* animals. However, most of the research has been conducted with dogs.

Studies of animal-assisted therapy show that the presence of a dog lessens feelings of loneliness, reduces the experience of physical pain, and lowers cortisol levels during stressful situations.

Many combat veterans utilize emotional-service animals to help them cope with stressful situations. Studies are currently being conducted to investigate the role that service dogs play in healing their owners from post-traumatic symptoms.

A study of children who had been sexually abused found that when a dog was present during their group therapy, the children "showed significant decreases in trauma symptoms including anxiety, depression, anger, post-traumatic stress disorder, dissociation, and sexual concerns" (Dietz, Davis, and Pennings 2012).

In many countries, including the United States, certified emotional-service animals are allowed to accompany their owners on airplanes and in hotels, stores, and other public places.

In addition, studies show that dog owners are twice as likely to engage in regular walks, compared to non–dog owners. These dog walks have been correlated with significant mental and physical health benefits. Walking your dog is also an excellent way to meet your neighbors or other animal lovers at the local dog park.

Having a dog or other pet can ease post-traumatic symptoms. When emotions are shut down after a trauma, loving a pet can help reawaken your feelings. You begin to care about someone—your pet—which is a great starting point for letting love in.

Programs that specialize in training service dogs for combat veterans report that their dogs can reduce hypervigilance from trauma. It's like having a second set of eyes to watch for possible danger, so the traumatized person can finally relax. You can find these services with an Internet search for "PTSD service dog."

In addition, pets can bring out a sense of playfulness in those who haven't been able to relax because of trauma.

On a personal note, I can attest to the calming power of a pet. Animals have a keen sense of what a person needs. When I was a child and awoke crying from nightmares, my fluffy orange cat, Mickey, would always run to me and cuddle with me until I fell back asleep.

Later in life, when I was going through a difficult situation, I adopted my first dog, Valentine. The moment I held her to my chest, I felt a sensation as if Valentine was healing and reopening my heart! The phrase *puppy therapy* came to my mind, as her comfort truly *was* therapeutic and gave me support until the stressful situation was resolved.

Then as my travel schedule felt increasingly stressful, I was able to qualify for a certified emotional-service dog. She accompanied me on many airplane flights and sat on my lap during workshops. Her presence definitely had a calming effect on me! (Come to think of it, I did *not* have my dog with me the day that I cried tears of stress in the Toronto airport, as I described in the Preface. Hmm . . .)

How to Be a Good Friend

We will be examining the personality characteristics of other people in this section; however, it's equally important to take a self-assessment and ask: *Am I a good friend?* Surveys show that close friendships are more equated with life happiness than marriage, so these relationships are very important to well-being.

Everyone's definition of a "good friend" is different, but there are basic characteristics that are reported in studies of friendship. They include:

- ✳ **Trustworthiness**. Keeping your promises and having integrity. This is especially important if your trust has been previously betrayed.

- ✳ **Protectiveness**. There's an unspoken code among friends that you'll protect each other. That includes defending your friends if you hear gossip about them, and helping them when they need it.

- ✳ **Confidentiality**. Never gossip about your friends or reveal their secrets to others.

- ✳ **Noncompetition.** While friendly competition during a sports game may be okay, striving to be "better" than your friend puts strain on the relationship.

- ✳ **Mutuality.** The conversations give both people time and attention to share. Each friend listens to the other.

- ✳ **Availability.** We're all busy, but good friends make time for each other.

All of these qualities help you feel safe and "at home" with your good friends.

Be aware of your post-traumatic personality tendencies, which could be unpleasant for your friends, such as the following:

— If you tend to be a **fighter**, then recognize when anger flares in your mind and body.

Healthy ways to handle this tendency: You may be having an emotional flashback and reacting to past trauma instead of the current situation. Walk away for a moment to discharge the anger with action. Take some deep breaths. Speak only after you've cleared and centered your mind, to avoid saying something hurtful. If you do lash out with anger, be sure to apologize, take responsibility, and talk with your friend about what happened.

— If you tend to be **dramatic**, then recognize your tendency to panic and catastrophize situations that aren't really emergencies. High drama can upset other people, especially if you're loudly saying that there's some sort of danger everyone needs to take immediate action to defend against.

Healthy ways to handle this tendency: If you feel that urgency building within you, take a moment to discharge the energy through stretching exercises. Flex your arms, do some bends, take deep breaths, and release the anxiety. Try to do all this as undramatically as possible, or excuse yourself to the restroom, where you can stretch in private.

— If you tend to **dissociate**, then your friends may think you're uninterested in them when they notice your eyes have glazed over and you're only answering them with one-word replies.

Healthy ways to handle this tendency: Grounding yourself can keep you from drifting away. This means to put your conscious awareness upon your bodily sensations. Notice the feeling of your feet in your shoes, your back against the chair, and so forth. Notice any tension in your muscles. Notice whether your breath is shallow. The more you become aware of your body, the more present you are for your friends and for yourself.

— If you tend to be **codependent**, then you may overdo generosity toward your friends. You're so grateful to have friends that you express appreciation in over-the-top, elaborate ways. This may block you from receiving friendship in return, and you may become resentful that you're the one doing all the giving.

Healthy ways to handle this tendency: Remind yourself that when you allow your friends a chance to give to you, you are helping them to be happy, too. Practice balancing both giving and receiving daily.

In your friendships, stay aware of your physical and emotional feelings. Notice if you begin to emotionally escalate into fear or anger, and walk away to get clarity. Don't blame or burden yourself with other people's drama. You can care about them without hurting yourself with worry and stress.

All it takes is one good friendship for you to discover that you are lovable. Friendship takes time and commitment, but it's an investment that pays big dividends.

CHAPTER TWELVE

Choosing Your Friends Wisely

Part of self-care is using discernment when choosing with whom you spend time. As we've seen in the previous chapter, if you've been traumatized, you may tend to choose "safe" relationships where you're guaranteed to be accepted . . . usually because such relationships are with people whom you don't admire. They may be substance abusers or much further down the socioeconomic ladder than you. This relates to rescuing and trying to "fix up" people, under the guise that it's a selfless, compassionate act.

In the past, you may have chosen friends based upon your common trauma background or dysfunctional coping styles. Those forms of relationships are guaranteed to contain drama and emotional pain, unless you've both committed to working on yourselves.

Everyone has some issue they're working on, and as we've seen, the majority of people have experienced trauma. Researchers have concluded: "Epidemiologic studies show that . . . most people will experience a traumatic event at some point in their life, and up to 25% of them will develop [PTSD]" (Hidalgo and Davidson 2000).

Choose to surround yourself with people who are aware of their issues. You want to be with someone who has taken steps to deal with his or her "stuff," through psychotherapy, self-care regimens, and the like.

> Choose to be with people who are aware of their issues and who are taking healthful steps to deal with them.

How to Spot and Avoid Drama-Addicted Friends

As you detox from drama addiction, you may need to pull away (temporarily or permanently) from people who feed into the addiction. This is similar to a newly recovering alcoholic distancing him- or herself from previous drinking buddies.

While you can have compassion for everyone struggling with addictions, you've got to take strong measures to heal yourself. Pray for your friends who are still addicted, send them helpful articles and books if they're open to it . . . but don't allow their influence to pull you off your healthy course.

Here are some characteristics to avoid, especially in the beginning of your recovery from drama addiction. Stay away from people who:

✳ Obsessively and repeatedly talk about their problems, without any interest in solutions

✳ Break their promises

✳ Act and speak dramatically, in an exaggerated, animated way

✳ Treat others disrespectfully

✳ Have one-sided conversations—always about being special, either especially wonderful or especially un-lucky

✳ Speak loudly and rapidly

✳ Currently abuse drugs or alcohol

✳ Frequently fish for compliments

✳ Brag about breaking the law

✳ Have "doomsday" fears about the end of the world

✳ Constantly express anger about a wide variety of issues

✳ Frequently use exaggeration words like *always* and *never*

✳ Have unfocused eyes that aren't looking at you

✳ Talk *at* you or *to* you, not *with* you

✳ Only contact you when they want something from you

✳ Brag about how much stress they're under, like it's a badge of courage

✳ Boast about being a victim, subject to other people's will

✳ Gossip about others (they will do the same about you)

✳ Can cite every detail about every celebrity's life

✳ Are incessantly complaining about how much they have to do

✳ Are in the habit of telling wild stories about themselves or people they know

As you get stronger in your recovery from stress and drama, you'll be in a better position to help other drama-addicted people to recognize the stress cycle that they're in. But in the beginning, it's best to avoid their company as much as is practical (we'll discuss how to deal with negative family members in Chapter 14).

Your Inner Warning Signals

Your body is innately sensitive to other people's energies and intentions. After enduring trauma, you become even more tuned in to people around you as a protective measure. However, you may ignore your inner warning signals, which you later regret.

Part of your self-care, then, is to notice—and most of all, trust, listen to, honor, and follow—your inner warning signals. They may come to you as tightened muscles, as a feeling that something's wrong, or as a knowingness that you can't trust a certain person or that he or she isn't a positive companion for you. However you receive these signals is perfect, as long as you notice and follow them.

When you're with friends or new acquaintances, check your own inner warning signals, which will alert you that you're with a drama-addicted person:

- ✳ You feel bored and anxious, because he or she tells the same stories repeatedly.

- ✳ You feel used, because it's a one-sided relationship, with you doing all the giving.

- ✳ You have a desire to avoid the person.

- ✳ You feel that you're wasting your time being with him or her.

- ✳ You have somatic reactions to being in his or her presence, such as bodily pain or illness.

- ✳ You feel guilty, like you owe the person something.

- ✳ You feel angry at him or her and at yourself.

- ✳ After the person leaves, you feel drained and tired.

These warning signals largely won't be there in a healthy friendship. If one or two of the signals arise, in a healthy relationship you'll feel comfortable facing and working through them.

If your traumatic experience has left you feeling unworthy, or afraid of people, then you'll need to move slowly and gently with friendships. Easy does it.

Remember that it's not the *quantity* of friends you have that's important; it's the *quality* of the relationships. True friendship is worth the time and energy it takes to develop.

Stress-Hormone Addiction and Personality

When I was studying personality disorders in college, my professors warned us students to beware of "Psych 101 Syndrome." This is a tendency in those who are studying psychological diagnoses to believe that they have all of the listed symptoms. So read the following section from an objective perspective, and know that this isn't necessarily describing you. Most personality disorders are extreme cases of normal characteristics, in people whose lives and happiness are limited by these attributes.

The main characteristic of personality disorders is an extreme difficulty in maintaining healthy relationships. In truth, those fitting these descriptions are lonely, hurt, and angry. But they isolate themselves from further hurt by reducing other people to objects, and by putting up a wall of self-centeredness and anger.

Psychotherapist Pete Walker, author of *Complex PTSD*, theorizes that the four different trauma responses (*fight, flight, freeze,* and *fawn*) can result in four personality disorders (or a combination of them):

* **Fight** results in *narcissism*, and trying to keep safe through power and control.

* **Flight** results in *obsessive-compulsive disorder*, and trying to keep safe through perfectionism.

* **Freeze** results in *dissociative states*, and trying to keep safe through isolation.

* **Fawn** results in *codependency*, and trying to keep safe by making others happy.

Feeling Loved Equals Feeling Safe

I would adjust Walker's model by adding that not only are we trying to feel safe; we are trying to feel *loved* (which makes us feel safe, valued, and secure). All of these personality modes are attempts to control the feeling of being loved, rather than *allowing* love into our hearts, minds, and lives.

Feeling loved relieves the existential angst that causes us to wonder, *Why am I here?* Love justifies and validates our very existence, and heals any feelings that our presence has been a stressful nuisance to our parents and the planet. Love makes us glad to be alive.

The narcissist and codependent try to control other people, the dissociative tries to control his or her consciousness, and the obsessive-compulsive attempts to control his or her environment . . . all in an attempt to feel loved—which never works, because control is based upon fear, not love.

✳   ✳   ✳

Here are descriptions of the personality issues associated with trauma symptoms.

If you relate to any of these descriptions, know that these are about personality, not mental illness. Help is available to relieve the anxiety beneath these issues, and these descriptions can help you identify issues within your relationships as well.

NARCISSISM

We usually think of a narcissist as someone who is self-obsessed and vain. In addition, though, narcissists are often adrenaline addicts who fuel their high by creating constant drama. They believe that their problems are special crises and

demand that everyone stop what they are doing and participate in the unfolding drama.

Underlying the narcissist is repressed anger (the "fight"
reaction to trauma) and a fear of abandonment. This often
manifests as boredom when life seems too ordinary and calm.
Narcissists need constant attention and validation, and having
a crisis puts them in the spotlight. They also push away emotionally intimate relationships with their anger.

Narcissists can heal this cycle by facing their feelings of anger, fears of abandonment, and low self-worth in a supportive
therapeutic setting.

Obsessive-Compulsive Disorder

We often think of obsessive-compulsive behavior as endless hand washing or another repetitive behavior to assuage
negative thoughts. Yet it's so much more, especially when
there's a history of trauma.

Obsession means a recurring feeling or thought. *Compul-
sion* means an impulse to perform an action that the person
feels no control over. The obsessive thoughts and feelings are
a fear that if the compulsive action isn't executed, something
bad will happen.

The fear is generalized, but it can become specific (for example, *If I don't look perfect, no one will find me attractive or love
me,* or *I must put on my right shoe first or I'll have a bad day*). Like
most phobias, these beliefs are often based upon past stressful experiences (such as a personal tragedy occurring on a day
when the person put on his or her left shoe first). A connection
was made and became an obsession with a compulsive ritual.

Obsessive-compulsive behavior usually involves supersti-
tious rituals, called *atonements,* to magically undo guilt or fear.

For example, going to sleep may involve a series of compulsive behaviors such as the lights being turned out in a certain order, the pillows and comforters folded in a specific way, and so on. These rituals become very rigid, and if another person disrupts the routine, it creates a lot of upset.

Obsessive-compulsive people also have rigid opinions about what's right or wrong, as well as high moral standards and ethics. They can come across as supremely judgmental, which pushes people away. Ironically, although they hold others to high standards, they may violate these standards themselves, with excuses to justify their behavior.

Research also links the obsessive-compulsive behavior known as "hoarding" to trauma and life stress (Landau 2010). Hoarding means that a person collects multiple items or pets, to their own detriment financially, space-wise, or even in terms of health (especially for hoarded pets).

Obsessive-compulsive personality disorder stems from the flight response to trauma, with a desire to run away from fear and pain. Obsessive-compulsive behavior involves physically or mentally fleeing from the *awareness* of emotional pain by continually rushing around and trying to perfectly accomplish an endless list of tasks. Obsessive-compulsive people believe that as long as they stay busy, they don't have to think about or feel anything painful. As a result, they often act out the workaholism addiction, until they realize the harm this pattern does to themselves and their loved ones.

DISSOCIATIVE STATES

If you were trapped in an overwhelmingly frightening or painful situation, then you didn't have the opportunity to fight back or run away. So you "escaped" mentally by your consciousness losing awareness of the situation. You were physically there, with your muscles tightening into a freeze state, braced for the pain. But like in an out-of-body experience, your mind was somewhere else.

In extreme cases of ongoing abuse, there can be such a permanent dissociation that multiple personalities are created. Two of the psychiatric hospitals I worked at focused upon multiple personalities, so I learned firsthand how this splitting of consciousness is created as a coping mechanism during abusive situations.

In less extreme cases, dissociation is more along the lines of losing track of time, forgetting how you arrived somewhere, and living in a fantasy world that's out of touch with reality. It can also include constantly daydreaming, or escaping through fantasy in novels, television, or movies.

You'll know you're with a person who dissociates when there's a feeling he or she is not listening to you, his or her eyes are glazed over and voice is monotone, and you can sense that he or she is "not present" with you.

Codependency:
People-Pleasing and Buying Love

If you feel unworthy of love or friendship, you may overdo it by trying to "win" other people's love with gifts or money or by doing favors for them. This will usually result in people being with you, but not because they like you.

Codependency is often created through the "fawn" state of experiencing a trauma. Similar to the famous "Stockholm syndrome," in which prisoners begin sympathizing with their captors, fawning means that you try to control painful relationships by pleasing the other person.

With codependency, you learn how to tune in to other people's feelings so you'll know what to say or do to win their approval. This puts you out of touch with your own feelings, though.

Plus, you'll only attract "takers" with this one-way giving style. People pleasers often have flocks of takers around them. No wonder people pleasers feel lonely! After all, they haven't shown anyone their vulnerable side of being unhappy. They instead pretend to always be delighted to help, when inside they're praying that someone will give to them for once.

If you try to buy love with your money or by rescuing others, then don't be surprised later that they only love you for your money or what you can do for them. And don't be surprised if—when you stop giving them everything—those people leave your life.

True friendship requires an investment of time and energy (on both people's part).

✳   ✳   ✳

In addition to these four trauma-related personalities as identified by Walker, post-traumatic research finds that avoidant personality (which was described earlier) often results from unhealed trauma, as well as histrionic and borderline personalities.

HISTRIONIC PERSONALITY

Similar to narcissism, histrionic personality means a constant need to draw attention to oneself. This person is usually seductive, provocative, and emotionally shallow.

In conversation, the histrionic person exaggerates for the sake of attention, using words like *always* and *never* a lot. These individuals are frequently labeled "drama queens," because they overreact to everything and assume that worst-case scenarios will occur.

Like narcissists, histrionic people repress a lot of anger and a sense that they are a victim in a special way. Histrionic people often bait others into dramatic arguments.

BORDERLINE PERSONALITY

Borderline personality occurs when a person has a pervasive pattern of instability in relationships, self-image, and behavior. Such a person doesn't know who he or she is and has no sense of identity, changing tastes and opinions according to the people and circumstances surrounding him or her.

There's a strong correlation between having post-trauma symptoms and a borderline personality, because both can arise from prolonged childhood trauma. People are desperately searching for themselves; however, they usually are looking for a person or situation to be the one "magic key" that will end their search. Only when they realize that external searches are futile do they finally begin the healing process of looking within and discovering themselves.

The preceding descriptions are called "personality disorders," because the psychological model equates the word *disorder* with the need for treatment. This makes sense—but still, calling someone "disordered" can be disempowering. Perhaps think of the word *disorder* like you would a closet that isn't orderly. Personality disorders do mean a disheveled and disorganized approach to life.

You may recognize yourself in these descriptions, which is helpful information to address. The healing methods described in Part II of this book are very effective for reducing the anxiety underlying these personality issues.

Can This Friendship Be Healed?

If you recognize yourself or your friends in this chapter, that's understandable. After all, we tend to flock to like-minded people, so if you've been traumatized, you would be drawn to others with similar experiences.

There's also a lock and key with respect to personality-issue matches. For instance, narcissists, who want to control everyone, are often attracted to codependents, who want to make everyone happy. The trouble is, the codependent becomes the slave to the narcissist, believing this will make him or her happy. Since the narcissist is inherently *un*happy, the codependent never gets the payoff of making someone else happy. So, the two dysfunctions grow apart from each other.

Healthy relationships (as we'll discuss in the next chapter) comprise two people who are aware of, and willing to work on, their emotional issues. Everyone has some personal issue to learn from and improve. However, those who get defensive and won't look at their issues are emotionally stagnant. Their fears of looking inward keep them from true happiness and intimacy.

There are lovingly assertive ways to discuss someone's emotional issues, which opens the door to sharing feelings. Aggressive accusations slam the door shut.

Own your feelings in the discussion, such as "I feel [name of emotion] when [example of actions triggering this feeling]."

This is much better than accusing, like: "You make me so mad!"

When someone is accused or blamed, he or she shuts down and can't hear what you're saying. This is especially true when that person is hypersensitive because of trauma.

For example, if your friend is chronically late to meet you, you could say: "I feel abandoned and disrespected when you don't show up at the time that we agreed upon, and I don't like those feelings." And then discuss solutions and alternatives so that it doesn't happen again.

Don't make threats or ultimatums, unless you are prepared to back them up with action.

If you're conflict-phobic, then having an honest discussion will help you to face and overcome that fear. Friendships can grow closer as the two people work together to overcome issues.

CHAPTER THIRTEEN

Sparkling Romantic Relationships

L et me begin this chapter by saying that I've learned much of this the hard way. Although I have taken undergraduate and graduate psychology courses, including all the courses required to be a marriage and family counselor, I learned more from *being* in unhealthy relationships.

My parents, married since they were teenagers (going on 60 years now), have one of those ideal "best friend" romantic relationships that most of us dream of. They adore each other. So my standards were high for a marriage, and it hurt me when I couldn't seem to meet them. Finally, I realized that finding true love began with finding the love within *me*.

Searching Endlessly for Love and Fulfillment

If you crave being loved in a relationship that's safe and mutually respectful, these are normal human desires. You deserve to have those qualities in your relationships. We all do!

If your love life has been one disappointment after another, this is probably because of a need for the starting point of self-love. You've repeatedly heard the adage "You can't love someone else until you love yourself." Yet, we're all a work in progress in learning this lesson. Very few have mastered the art of complete self-acceptance.

If you can begin with caring about whether you feel happy or not and being concerned if you're in emotional pain, that's a great jumping-off point. When you care about yourself, you'll arrange your life so that *you* are cared for. You won't settle for relationships with people who treat you shabbily and who don't care about you.

In every moment of every relationship, we are always teaching the other person how we want to be treated. This is called "boundaries," meaning your deal breakers—what you will and won't accept.

Without self-love, you'll accept the first person who shows you attention, regardless of how that person *treats* you. You'll be more concerned about whether the person likes you, rather than if *you* like the other person. You'll focus upon how your heart pounds and you feel butterflies around the object of your affection, instead of wondering whether you get excited because your chemistry is reacting to meeting another dysfunctional person.

Is this someone you're attracted to mentally, emotionally, and spiritually? Is it just a physical attraction? Excitement at the prospect of rescuing or changing this person? Or desperation to not be alone?

If you've chosen past romantic partners based upon the chemistry you felt, how did that work for you? If it didn't, this is a sign that your potential-partner radar has its dial set to *dysfunction*.

This is usually because we pick up on unconscious signals that a new person has the same dysfunctions as one of our parents. It's a deep-seated desire to change that parent into someone who makes us feel loved. When our new romantic partner can't fulfill that fantasy, because his or her heart is closed due to unhealed trauma symptoms, we are disappointed once again.

With self-love, in contrast, you'll take your time to get to know the person before you fully commit. You'll check into your own feelings to see if this person could add to your emotional, intellectual, and spiritual growth. If you notice red-flag warnings (lack of ethics or self-awareness, for instance, or a tendency to blame everyone else or a substance-abuse issue), you'll extricate yourself from the relationship rather than getting more involved.

Addictive Relationships

If you have a tendency toward addictions, you may have an "addictive personality." This is an inclination to overdo everything in an attempt to feel better. You may also have a genetic predisposition toward alcoholism or drug abuse (if a relative also had those issues).

For those who are prone to addictions, even a little alcohol or drugs can have an emotional impact and shut their hearts. People who are overwhelmed with life, feeling it's all too painful, will often numb themselves with chemicals.

If you are in a relationship with a substance abuser (alcohol or drugs), your love needs won't be met. The person is not capable of giving you the love that you desire (and *deserve*) because his or her own emotions are chemically numbed.

Even more, when people are high, drunk, or hungover, they often do and say things that they wouldn't when sober. These dramatic escapades can lead to a roller coaster of relationship woes, including multiple breakups with the same person.

Addictive love also includes serial dating, where you're so afraid of being alone and so desperate to feel loved that you'll connect with anyone. Brief relationships and one-night stands are based in addictive love.

If the addictions begin to interfere with your career, income, reputation, health, or other necessary aspects of your life, then professional addiction help may be needed. Addictions-specific psychotherapy and support such as one of the 12-step programs are effective forms of help.

The Mr. Darcy Syndrome

I worked as an addictions therapist for many years, and I trust the process. So why did I experience painful relationships, with my background as a therapist and an intuitive person whose parents still have a healthy marriage? I should have known better, right?

Perhaps, like me in the past, you've been attracted to "bad boys" (or "bad girls"). This certainly is part of the trauma-drama-stress addiction cycle. Few things in life are more stressful than having a here-comes-trouble romantic partner.

In the Jane Austen novel *Pride and Prejudice*, Lizzie Bennet's heart pounds with excitement when she sees Mr. Darcy, who is scowling and ignoring her. Our hearts pound with romantic excitement along with her. Although Mr. Darcy later softens and warms up, in real life, most bad boys and girls continue their defensive *I-don't-care-what-you-think* attitude in romantic relationships.

So why are we attracted to bad boys and girls? Researchers say that heterosexual women are attracted to tough guys because of our ancient need to have a strong provider and protector.

WHY ARE WE ATTRACTED TO BAD BOYS AND GIRLS?

In addition, relationships with bad boys or girls provide variable reinforcement, much like a casino slot machine. You never know when the relationship will reward you with romance or deliver ice-cold punishment. This leads to an addiction to the toxic relationship.

Bad boy/girl interactions are psychologically abusive because you usually blame yourself for your partner's negative mood or detachment. If that person also abuses drugs or alcohol (which is so often the case with bad boys and girls), the relationship becomes even more combustible.

Our feel-good brain chemical dopamine is released when situations are unpredictable, such as a drama-filled relationship. So, it's part of the hypervigilance of post-trauma. In addition, dopamine is released when we anticipate a possible reward, like taming a bad boy or girl. That's why getting excited about something occurring in the future is an addictive experience.

Researchers also find that we all have an innate belief that the more difficult something is to obtain, the more valuable it is. At some level, we all love a challenge. So, this makes us ignore that nice-but-predictable guy or gal who wants to love us, in favor of the unpredictable and unreliable bad boy or girl . . . until we get hurt enough times and learn to value a stable and reliable relationship.

There's also a deep-seated belief that a safe and predictable relationship is boring. So, you meet a "nice guy" or "nice gal" and you yawn with disinterest, and move on to the person who makes your heart race.

This physical and energy connection is called "chemistry," but if your love radar is set to only be activated by unattainable and uncaring people, then chemistry is *not* the way for you to define compatibility.

Those who've been traumatized often overlook warning signals when they meet someone new. A bad temper, a history of violence, and harsh speech are signs that you're meeting a potential abuser. Yet, if you've shut down your feelings, you may disregard these danger signals . . . or even feel excited by them.

In addition, abusers are experts at pretending to be gentle as a way of seducing others. That's why it's essential to take all relationships slowly, until you can get to know the real person. Ask the person why his or her last relationship ended, and really listen to the answer. If you hear him or her blaming the other person and taking no responsibility for the relationship troubles, that's a sign that *you* will be blamed in the future.

R.E.S.P.E.C.T.

Mutual respect is essential to a happy, healthy, long-term relationship. A study found that couples who treated each other with disrespect were apt to spend more time apart following an argument than mutually respectful couples. Respecting each other is a way to communicate honestly and get past arguments and into healing.

Respect for the process of communicating is essential, not only to the relationship but also to the health of both partners. A study of "arguing styles" in couples found that when one partner shut down and dissociated from the conversation or walked away, both partners suffered physically. Increased stress hormones, hurt feelings of rejection, and blood-pressure changes were the harmful results.

Respect goes both ways. If you're healing from trauma symptoms, you'll need to be aware of—and contain—any acting-out anger tendencies toward your romantic partner.

Anytime two or more people gather, there are bound to be differences of opinions. It's not *whether* you have conflict, but how you *handle* it that matters.

Why It's Better to Be Alone Than in an Unhealthy Relationship

One reason why we settle for unhealthy relationships is the fear of being alone. The great philosopher and mathematician Blaise Pascal said it best: "All of humanity's problems stem from man's inability to sit quietly in a room alone." This is true of both men and women, and probably children, too.

Why is it difficult to be alone? The main reason is that you haven't developed a best-friend relationship with yourself. If you . . .

✳ Keep your promises to yourself

✳ Take good care of your body

✳ Don't betray yourself

✳ Don't push yourself beyond your energy levels

✳ Rest when you need to

✳ Have fun

※ Give yourself gifts

※ Offer yourself sincere compliments

※ Spend your time in meaningful ways

. . . then you will be treating yourself as you'd like a best friend to treat you. You will enjoy spending time alone if you enjoy your own company and are nice to yourself—just as you enjoy the companionship of others who are nice to you.

Being alone is preferable to being in an unhealthy relationship filled with hostile drama, especially if your partner refuses to look at his or her issues, or won't accompany you to therapy.

If children are involved in the partnership, they benefit from being away from the arguing and unhappiness. Just be sure to work on the inner reasons why you got into that relationship in the first place, or you'll end up in another relationship with identical dysfunctional dynamics.

Where Is He (She)?

If you're currently single, with a desire to be in a healthy romantic relationship, you may wonder where to meet an emotionally functional partner.

First, be sure you are dealing with the underlying issues that drove you to be in unhealthy relationships previously. Make certain you're not putting all the blame for your previous relationships on your ex-partners. Unless you were in an arranged marriage, *you* were the one who chose that partner or agreed to be with him or her.

Taking responsibility for your previous choices isn't to blame yourself, either. Blame and guilt are never helpful, but understanding the reasons behind your choices is essential. This information helps you understand yourself and increases the chances that you won't repeat that pattern.

You'll know if you're ready for healthy love by watching your actions. If you continue to be attracted to unavailable, addicted, or otherwise inappropriate partners, that's a sign that you're not quite "cooked" and ready to come out of the oven yet. Back to therapy you go.

You're like a rose that will bloom when the time is right. You can't forcibly try to open your petals of relationship readiness. In fact, if you are desperate for love, that's a sign of underlying fears that need to be addressed.

It's unhealthy to look for a partner who will fix your life. That approach will only attract a codependent rescuer, and you won't have your love needs met in such a fear-based relationship. Instead, you need to first rescue yourself . . . so that you can be in a *love*-based (not fear-based) relationship with a healthy partner.

So take this time as a single to repair whatever needs fixing in your life: pay off your financial debts, get your career going, do forgiveness work, take care of your body, and so forth. You'll feel much better about yourself, and your new confidence will be attractive to an emotionally secure romantic partner.

We all have fears of being hurt. The question is: what will you *do* with these fears? *Healthy* says: "I will notice and understand the fears, but I won't let them control me." *Unhealthy* says: "I won't take the risk of being hurt, including not risking looking at my fears because that would reveal to me potentially painful truths."

So, your choices in romantic partners are like a "canary in a coal mine" that signal your readiness or not. Although in the beginning of a relationship, you may believe that your intended is wonderful, it takes about six months of dating for a person to drop his or her guard and show his or her true colors.

Your friends can probably see the true person in your potential partner. If they give you warnings about who you're dating, listen! You may assume they are jealous and want to burst your romantic bubble. But if they've shown you genuine friendship in the past, trust that their warnings are part of being a good friend. Trust them!

In fact, friends are the best way to meet new potential partners. A survey of long-term married people showed that the majority met through friends. This makes sense, because you share common interests with your friends, so you'd also share common elements with *their* friends. So throw a party and ask your friends to bring along their other friends (including eligible siblings, too).

As with meeting healthy friends, you can meet potential partners at classes, groups, and clubs (not nightclubs) related to your interests. It's a matter of overcoming social anxieties enough to attend these gatherings, and then having the courage to smile and say "hello." Even if you don't see a potential love mate at these groups, you may make a wonderful new friend. And who knows? That new friend's sibling may be your healthy love match!

CHAPTER FOURTEEN

How to Be Yourself with Your Family Members

The number one question I received after the publication of my book *Assertiveness for Earth Angels* was: "How can I deal with my hurtful family members?" This chapter will answer that question.

Post-traumatic stress is often passed down through family generations. As an example, if your great-grandfather was traumatized by military combat, he may have withdrawn emotionally from his wife (your great-grandmother) and their son (your grandfather). Then your grandfather, who received little contact with his father, grew up to be emotionally distant as well. This affected your father, and now it affects *you*.

In addition, you can become traumatized by listening to gruesome details from family members discussing their trauma. A European study on this topic concluded: "The presence of posttraumatic stress disorder (PTSD) in male war veterans has been linked with family dysfunction and psychopathology in their children" (Maršanić et al. 2014).

This is an important reason for adults to be very discerning when discussing trauma in front of children, and not let them watch news videos of disasters. If children *are* exposed to this material, a responsible adult should help them process and make sense of the traumatic information.

Fighting with Ghosts from the Past

When you've been traumatized, you can have an emotional flashback and dissociation that has you reliving a past relationship pattern, as if it's happening now. If you feel like your family relationships are recurring nightmares, it's likely because you're fighting with fragments of the past. The arguments are on automatic pilot, and no one is really present or conscious at the moment. This is especially true when your family members exhibit post-traumatic symptoms as well. In these cases, it's a group flashback in the form of an argument.

As trauma expert Bessel van der Kolk, M.D., writes:

> A person whose fundamental preoccupation is to be ready for the next assault is also likely to generate a constant torrent of thoughts related to survival. This may range from obsessive rage against real and imaginary assailants to relentless worrying about having provoked rejection and abandonment. (van der Kolk 2011)

It's almost akin to hallucinating attacks coming your way. Unfortunately, what you expect is often what you create or attract.

If you were also traumatized, you may join a family member's ongoing fixation on "the world is against me." The question is: do you meet that person in this unreal attack fantasy because your own traumatic background is creating dissociation, or do you truly help the person by talking him or her off the ledge that exists only in the mind? The answer is for you to take the path that is healthiest for yourself. As you get stronger and regain your sparkle, you can better help others do the same.

When Our Feelings Get Hurt

We can try to soothe our feelings with the adages "We can't control other people's reactions, only our reaction to them," and "Don't take anything personally, because their actions are a reflection on themselves, not on you."

These refrains help us intellectualize the other person's actions, which can be helpful.

Still, the stinging barb of harsh words or actions can bypass our intellect and go straight to our emotions, which are *hurt* by unkindness, unless we've numbed ourselves with chemicals, food, or dissociation . . . and we don't want to handle feelings in unhealthy ways any longer!

So let's explore how to keep your heart open and feel emotions, while safeguarding against overwhelming emotional pain.

THE SCIENCE OF HURT FEELINGS

Many scientific (physiological) and psychological studies have attempted to measure and understand hurt feelings. There's even a scientific definition of hurt feelings from Mark Leary, Ph.D., a professor at Duke University who has studied the topic extensively:

Perceived relational devaluation (or low relationship evaluation); that is, the target [the person with hurt feelings] per-
ceives that the offender regards the relationship as less valuable, important, or close than the target would like. (Leary
and Springer 2000)

So if someone in your family says or does something that
you interpret as devaluing your importance, it hurts! The key
word here is *interpret,* because as the scientists agree, "hurt feelings result from the target's interpretation of the partner's actions."

You certainly don't want to stuff down your hurt feelings.
After all, receiving emotional abuse is correlated with having a
weakened immune system. Scientists believe that many people
die prematurely because of the health-debilitating effects of
receiving emotional abuse.

What Is Emotional Abuse?

Also known as psychological, verbal, or mental abuse,
emotional abuse is the condition where you are repeatedly
hurt by being on the receiving end of the following on an
ongoing basis:

✳ **Put-downs**. Name-calling, cursing, and being told
that you're not good enough and that there's something wrong with you (including implying this or
jokingly making this accusation).

✳ **Manipulations**. Having attention, affection, or approval withheld until you comply with the person's
wishes. Playing cruel mind games with you.

✳ **Threats.** The other person threatening to harm you or a loved one in some way, if you don't comply with his or her wishes. This can also include the person threatening to hurt him- or herself and saying that it will be your fault.

✳ **Exploitation.** The other person using you for his or her own needs (such as pushing you to work while he or she lives off your income; prodding you to do something illegal, immoral, or against your beliefs for his or her own gain; or stealing from you).

✳ **Blaming.** The other person saying or implying that everything is your fault.

✳ **Overpowering.** Being intimidated by a loud barrage of angry words, until you submit to his or her will.

If you've been traumatized, you're more likely to minimize the painful effects that emotional abuse has upon you. Although it doesn't leave physical bruises, verbal abuse definitely creates mental and emotional scars. You feel unloved, controlled, and trapped. The constant put-downs and manipulations create an unhealthy atmosphere of fear that no one can, or should, live with.

If you recognize a current relationship as being emotionally abusive, it's essential to get support from a therapist, group therapy, or a domestic-violence hotline. It's not about changing the abusive person; it's about keeping *you* safe and healthy.

Dealing with Rudeness

Rudeness is associated with narcissistic and obsessive-compulsive personality issues. As you'll recall, narcissists are stuck in the "fight" mode. They are harboring anger from the pain of their trauma and want to lash out at the world . . . which includes you. They also want to control everyone to prevent further trauma, acting on their underlying fear of being unloved and abandoned.

Obsessive-compulsive individuals are stuck in the "flight" mode due to the trauma. Their trauma-related fears have been generalized, and there's an unconscious belief that if they had been "perfect," the trauma wouldn't have occurred. So they're obsessed with perfection in themselves, their homes . . . and also their friends and family, because of a belief that perfection will keep everyone safe. That's where the rudeness comes in, which is their misguided way of relating to other people.

Narcissists aren't aware of others' feelings or reactions to their controlling and angry ways, nor do they really care. They're like infants, only focused upon having their own fears comforted.

Obsessive-compulsives do care about others' feelings, but only because they're like school grades, demonstrating whether they're perfect or not. If they discover they've hurt your feelings, they're wounded and afraid, because this shows they're *not* perfect . . . and therefore, are vulnerable and unsafe. They also feel misunderstood, because in their minds, they were only trying to help *you* be safe by encouraging perfection.

Four Forms of Rudeness

According to extensive research from University of Louisville professor Michael Cunningham, Ph.D., there are four general forms of rudeness, which he calls "social allergens," because we're all emotionally allergic to and repelled by these behaviors:

1. **Uncouth habits.** Examples are loud gum chewing, burping, passing gas, and so forth, often intentionally directed at you. Unless the person is passive-aggressive (a passive-aggressive little brother may engage in these habits to annoy you), this form of rudeness is a product of either ignorance, unawareness, or uncaring. This is different from a person having an *unintentional* body reaction (burping or passing gas), especially if caused by illness.

2. **Egocentric actions.** The other person's actions violate your boundaries and show little regard for you, such as only talking about him- or herself (narcissism) and never asking about how *you* are.

3. **Norm violations.** These are behaviors that aren't directed at you but offend you nonetheless, such the people in the movie theater who talk nonstop.

4. **Intentional and personally directed rudeness.** This includes commanding you to do things, publicly putting you down, and other forms of verbal abuse.

When It's Your Family

The double bind that many people find themselves in is how to spend time with family when one or more members are rude or abusive. On the one hand, you have to save yourself from abuse, which is toxic to your mental, emotional, and physical health. But on the other hand . . . it's family! If you stay away, the guilt and sadness can be just as debilitating as the anger and hurt you feel when you're with them. Compounding these dynamics, you may be berated and ostracized for avoiding your family.

There are no one-size-fits-all solutions for these issues. Each relationship requires a different approach, depending upon:

✳ **Your tolerance for conflict.** Are you conflict-phobic, running from confrontation? Or do conflict and confrontation not bother you? (Watch out for conflict addiction as part of drama addiction, since discord elicits addictive stress hormones and dopamine.)

✳ **How guilt affects you.** Are you controlled by guilty feelings, or are you able to rise above them?

Your personal style will influence how you handle rudeness or abuse within your family.

Remember that the point isn't to change the other person or get him or her to apologize. The point is to help *you* deal with family dynamics in healthy ways. Although you crave feeling loved and appreciated by your family members, they may not be capable of fulfilling that need. Fantasizing that someday, under some condition, your family will change is a setup for disappointment.

REMEMBER THAT THE POINT ISN'T TO CHANGE THE OTHER PERSON OR GET HIM OR HER TO APOLOGIZE. THE POINT IS TO HELP *YOU* DEAL WITH FAMILY DYNAMICS IN HEALTHY WAYS.

So let's look at options for dealing with family members whose actions trigger hurt feelings, including the pros and cons of each method:

— **Distancing yourself:** You could move far away from them, and only visit via computer chats and every-other-year holiday get-togethers.

Pros: You're dealing with painful feelings, abuse, and/or drama less frequently.

Cons: You may miss your family members who aren't abusive or desire to protect an innocent family member who you know is getting equally hurt.

— **Confrontation:** Damn the torpedoes, because you're going to tell your family members precisely what you think about them.

Pros: You aren't holding on to your feelings, and others know exactly what you think and feel (even if they don't understand or agree with you).

Cons: Expressing anger isn't cathartic if you can't resolve the issue. Direct confrontation with an angry alcoholic or addict is potentially dangerous and can lead to physical abuse. Confrontation may shut down further communication and contact with family.

— **Assertiveness:** You express your feelings and thoughts in an assertive way (such as owning your feelings instead of blaming, and being calm, mature, and loving while talking).

Pros: Assertiveness helps you feel more confident in voicing your feelings. This method may help you overcome conflict phobia.

Cons: If you expect assertiveness to change the other person or elicit an apology, you'll feel disappointed.

— **Family therapy:** You and your family meet with a licensed psychotherapist to discuss and hopefully resolve your issues.

Pros: Having a supportive and trained neutral professional can facilitate communication in a safe environment.

Cons: Therapy can open up issues that can't be resolved in a 50-minute session. If insurance doesn't cover therapy, it can be expensive.

— **Family divorce:** You completely sever all contact. You never talk with or see any members of the family.

Pros: You don't have to worry about dealing with their conflicts in person.

Cons: You may still deal with family conflicts internally, unless you undergo therapy, attend support groups, or take other action to heal from painful family issues. You may miss some of the family members who weren't involved in the conflict.

Again, there's no right answer for everyone. Soul-searching, combined with support (such as a therapist or 12-step sponsor), can help you find answers to this challenging situation.

How to Keep Your Adult Identity During Family Visits

If you feel that you lose your adult identity when you're with your family, be sure to carry an object that reminds you of your current life and helps you feel empowered and proud of your accomplishments. Examples are a briefcase with work projects, a scholarly book you're reading, your favorite music recordings, or photos of you engaged in your current-life happenings.

In some cases, it's appropriate to bring something that lends emotional comfort to your inner child during a family visit, such as a small stuffed animal, a favorite blanket, or your pet dog. You may not want to flash your "blankie" or plush toy in front of your family, but you certainly could discreetly step into your car to hold your comfort item while your feelings are soothed.

If you live with people who have PTSR and anger issues, be sure to minimize the amount of histamine food and beverages in the house. Avoid alcohol, which is metaphorically throwing gasoline on the fire. I have a couple of distant relatives whom I stopped socializing with because they had a Jekyll-and-Hyde transformation the moment they began drinking wine. Out would come the insults, and away I'd go. I only see these relatives at locations that don't serve alcohol or at my house, because they're pretty nice people when they're sober.

If issues arise with your in-laws, it's natural for you to want your spouse to protect you. This may put you in a difficult position if he or she sides with family because of loyalty or fear, or if he or she remains passive and won't come to your defense.

It's unrealistic to ask your spouse to sever contact with his or her family. However, *you* certainly can . . . or at least, you can minimize contact. Tell in-laws you're busy that day, and then use the free time to work on your priorities.

When you have disapproving in-laws, it's very important to not try too hard to impress them. Those who try too hard are viewed with even more censure by disapproving people! So relax, be yourself, and detach from the need for their approval—and then you'll probably find that they *will* come around to you.

You have many choices for dealing with hurt feelings, including using rationalizations to detach and telling yourself, *Well, it's just their issues;* or having compassion because trauma has driven them out of their minds. Or you can cry cathartically, or be assertive, or never see them again. All are valid choices.

But any way you slice it, the situation will bring up stress hormones in your brain and body, and part of being responsible is taking care of yourself. So, go do yoga as soon as you can. Play gentle music, meditate, eat a low-histamine diet, and avoid chemicals.

CHAPTER FIFTEEN

Developing Healthy Relationships

As someone who's been traumatized, you may feel that you're different or "less than" people whom you consider to be normal and high functioning. Sometimes, this is because you compare how you feel on the inside with the way someone *appears* to be on the outside. This comparison isn't fair to you, because the other person who seems to have his or her act together may actually be struggling with insecurities.

Or perhaps you've been teased or verbally abused and called names that led to you feeling bad about yourself, like there's something fundamentally wrong with you.

Feeling socially awkward, shy, and sensitive can make it challenging to engage in new friendships and then maintain them. If you expect rejection, you're not likely to initiate contact with a friend. If you don't feel good about yourself, you're hesitant to begin a conversation with a new person.

Well, you *are* worthy and deserving of healthy friendships. We all are! You have a lot of love to give and receive, which is the basis of healthy relationships.

> YOU *ARE* WORTHY AND DESERVING OF HEALTHY FRIEND-
> SHIPS.

A healthy friendship will *add* to your life and provide you with comfort, love, and support. Of course, anytime two or more people are gathered, conflict could possibly arise. But in a healthy relationship, the conflict is handled with love and honesty until it is resolved.

Studies show that spending time with friends reduces the effects of aging and increases life satisfaction and positive mood. We are social animals who need human companionship.

The key is to choose friends who add a positive element to your life, and with whom you can reciprocate a healthy relationship. Research reveals that we tend to choose friends who are similar to ourselves, even to the point of sharing similar biological attributes. So, if you have low self-esteem, you're likely to be attracted to other people who also suffer from self-worth issues.

As mentioned earlier, if someone is aware of and working on his or her issues (and you are, too), there is great hope for a healthy relationship. With awareness, you can be honest with each other about conflicts, without defensiveness. That's because defensiveness is the opposite of awareness. It's the *refusal* to look at one's own issues out of fear of what will be discovered about oneself.

Sensitive people are often targets for those who mistake kindness for weakness. My book *Assertiveness for Earth Angels* is all about this topic. Since trauma has led you to become more sensitive, you'll need to be aware of the red flags when you're meeting new people.

If your previous friendship patterns have been dysfunctional and they pulled you down, then it will take a conscious effort on your part to know that you deserve better. We all do. Instead of connecting with people who are unaware of their issues, you'll make a commitment to be with people who are working on themselves.

One way to begin is to write a list of the qualities you'd like to have in a friend, such as someone who is:

✳ Caring

✳ A good listener

✳ Appreciative

✳ Loyal

✳ Honest

✳ Spiritually minded

✳ Working to improve his or her life

Lists of desirable traits are helpful in directing your focus when you meet new people, and you're less likely to get pulled back into old relationship habits. So, if you commit to only befriending honest people, you won't ignore someone bragging about how he or she lied or broke the law. You'll notice this discrepancy and say to yourself, *This person's traits don't mesh with my desires for my friendships.* Then, you'll move on to finding and being with people whose ethics match yours. It's easier to stop an unhealthy relationship in the beginning than to wait until bonds have been formed.

Now, there's a difference between holding standards for your friendships and having *unrealistic expectations* that become blocks to intimacy. One way to avoid relationships is to hold perfectionistic ideals for your friends and family, standards no one can meet, thereby ensuring that you'll stay alone.

There are no perfect people, only people who are either (1) aware of their issues and are actively working on self-improvement, or (2) unaware of their issues and unwilling to look at or work on them.

Where and How to Meet Healthful Friends

We gravitate toward people we can relate to, with whom we share common elements. In the past, you may have unknowingly bonded with people with whom you shared drama-addiction tendencies. You may have connected over the emotional wounds you had in common.

Were you surprised when the relationship was centered around drama and negativity? Did you spend all of your time listening to each other's latest problem? Aren't you tired of that activity?

Studies show that when we constantly talk about our problems with our friends, it leads to depression, which disempowers us from working on solutions. It's healthy to talk about our feelings with our friends, but not if it's a steady pity-party conversation about why we're a victim with no chance of bettering the situation.

To form healthy friendships means finding healthy people. And where do healthy people hang out? At *healthy* places!

Healthy places are locations where you can be actively involved in beneficial activities. For example:

- ✳ Yoga studios

- ✳ Gyms

- ✳ Healing centers

- ✳ Bookstores

- ✳ Spiritual centers

- ✳ Churches or temples

- ✳ Prayer vigils

- ✳ Dog parks

- ✳ Hiking trails

- ✳ Meditation classes

- ✳ Organic salons

- ✳ Charity events

- ✳ Healthful restaurants

- ✳ Eco-friendly stores

- ✳ Waldorf and Montessori schools, or progressive child-care facilities

I'm not saying that everyone you'll meet at these locations is emotionally healthy—far from it! However, your chances of finding compatible and healthy friendships is much higher if you connect at locations that are founded on self-improvement.

Classes are one of the best places for creating lasting friendships, because you're almost guaranteed to meet people who share common interests. Let's say that you've always wanted to learn more about photography, writing, scuba diving, or bicycling. There are clubs for these activities in almost every major city.

It's much easier to connect with someone when you meet in an ongoing, rather than a one-day, class. It usually takes everyone a day or two to release social inhibitions and nervousness. By day three, more intermingling occurs.

You can find these classes at your local college, adult-education center, or community center. Many classes are listed on international websites or meetup.com, or you can create your own and attract neighbors who share your interests. You'd be surprised how many interesting people live near you!

When you meet a new person, notice your bodily reactions. Do your muscles tighten in your jaw or stomach? This can be a sign that the person intimidates you.

Now probe further into this feeling, and notice whether you feel intimidated because the other person is throwing his or her "energy weight" around and being an "energy bully" (hogging all of the talking time or talking loudly, using harsh words or body language). Is there a sense that you and this person are competing with each other?

Or are you intimidated because you admire this person, and you feel out of his or her league? In these situations, it's helpful to recall how in the past it didn't work to befriend people whom you don't admire. You want and deserve friends who can lift you up and support you, not those who drag you down.

Remember, it's not about how many friends you have; it's the quality of the friendships that matters. Even one good friendship, built upon mutual respect and other healthy qualities, will help you sparkle throughout the day.

From Stressing to Stretching

Drama is an addictive habit with a physiological basis, just like other destructive addictions. The tragedy is that drama addiction is created during painful and frightening situations, and each new drama perpetuates the original trauma's ongoing harmful effects.

Fortunately, there is a healthy way out. First and foremost is being aware of your internal signals. When you become angry, frustrated, lonely, competitive, panicked, and so forth, observe yourself. Don't immediately react to these trauma-based habits.

As we've discussed, those who've been traumatized are more apt to have stressful experiences and react to those stressors in extreme ways. Knee-jerk automatic reactions to stress include the tendency to panic, dramatize, dissociate, try to control, and fight back. However, as the research shows, these patterns are ultimately unhealthy for your body and for your relationships.

There are life stressors that we can't control. Nevertheless, we *can* have control over our reactions to stress.

When you find yourself relapsing into dark yin or dark yang patterns (competitiveness, controlling, self-destructiveness, self-doubts, addictions, and the like), that's a signal to add more light to your life. Even when a dark mood convinces you that you don't deserve happiness or you feel that inner peace is impossible, it's essential to take action to restore your inner glow.

Taking action helps you discharge pent-up energy, especially if your original trauma resulted in a "freeze" response. Even small actions such as standing up and walking, or stretching your arms, will allow you to release pent-up emotions in healthful ways. This will reduce the levels of stress hormones in your body.

If you're upset, don't hold your feelings in or try to block awareness through addictive behaviors. Instead, take action to express your feelings in positive ways, such as writing song lyrics, journaling, exercising, painting, or dancing. Many successful creative people find that their darkest moments are inspiration for their songs, books, paintings, and such.

It also helps to write a letter to the person you're upset with. Pour out your feelings, and hold nothing back. Then, in a ceremonious way, burn the letter. You can also send a more restrained version of the letter to the person, after waiting a day or two for a cooling-off period. This way, your letter will reflect your ongoing feelings instead of reactive emotions.

So (1) notice your emotional and physical feelings, and then (2) take action to disperse and channel these feelings in productive—or at least nonharmful—ways.

Most important of all, please develop a personal relationship with your Creator. Talk with God like a best friend. Pray and ask for Divine intervention. Be open to listening to your positive inner guidance and following it without delay. After all, God created you as a Divine being of Light, and God will help you to retain and enjoy your Light—and shine it to inspire others.

As you've read throughout this book, almost all of us have been touched by traumatic circumstances. However, we don't need to let our past dictate our future. We can't allow the fear energy behind abusive situations to "win." We each need to take charge of our own health and happiness. And by doing so, we're also slowing or stopping the trauma-drama cycle around us. This is a major blessing to our loved ones and, ultimately, a contribution to our world.

When you sparkle, you inspire others to do the same. You become a candle bringing much-needed light to our world. Other people recognize your sparkle, even if they don't understand why. *Your* sparkle triggers a recollection within others that could be their catalyst for regaining their own.

So, sparkle on! And don't let *anything* dull your sparkle.

Bibliography

Abbaoui, B., Riedl, K. M., Ralston, R. A., Thomas-Ahner, J. M., Schwartz, S. J., Clinton, S. K., and Mortazavi, A. (2012 Nov). Inhibition of bladder cancer by broccoli isothiocyanates sulforaphane and erucin: Characterization, metabolism, and interconversion. *Mol Nutr Food Res*, 56(11), 1675–87.

Amsterdam, J. D., Li, Y., Soeller, I., Rockwell, K., Mao, J. J., and Shults, J. (2009 Aug). A randomized, double-blind, placebo-controlled trial of oral Matricaria recutita (chamomile) extract therapy for generalized anxiety disorder. *J Clin Psychopharmacol*, 29(4), 378–82.

Amsterdam, J. D., Shults, J., Soeller, I., Mao, J. J., Rockwell, K., and Newberg, A. B. (2012 Sep–Oct). Chamomile (Matricaria recutita) may provide antidepressant activity in anxious, depressed humans: An exploratory study. *Altern Ther Health Med*, 18(5), 44–9.

Araneta, M., Allison, M. A., Barrett-Connor, E., and Kanaya, A. M. (2013 June 22). Overall and regional fat change: Results from the Practice of Restorative Yoga or Stretching for Metabolic Syndrome (PRYSMS) study. Results presented at: 73rd Scientific Session of the American Diabetes Association in Chicago, IL.

Arora, S., and Bhattaharjee, J. (2008 Jul–Dec). Modulation of immune responses in stress by yoga. *Int J Yoga*, 1(2), 45–55.

Atsumi, T., and Tonosaki, K. (2007). Smelling lavender and rosemary increases free radical scavenging activity and decreases cortisol level in saliva. *Psychiatry Res*, 150, 89–96.

Bagga, O. P., and Gandhi, A. (1983 Jan–Feb). A comparative study of the effect of Transcendental Meditation (T.M.) and Shavasana practice on cardiovascular system. *Indian Heart Journal*, 35(1), 39–45.

Bayer-Topilsky, T., Trenerry, M. R., Suri, R., Topilsky, Y., Antiel, R. M., Marmor, Y., Mahoney, D. W., Schaff, H. V., and Enriquez-Sarano, M. (2013 Oct). Psycho-emotional manifestations of valvular heart diseases: Prospective assessment in mitral regurgitation. *Am J Med*, 126(10), 916–24.

Birnbaum, L. S. (2013 Jul). When environmental chemicals act like uncontrolled medicine. *Trends Endocrinol Metab*, 24(7), 321–3.

Boiten, F. A., Frijda, N. H., and Wientjes, C. J. E. (1994). Emotion and respiratory patterns: A review and critical analysis. *International Journal of Psychophysiology,* 17(2), 103–128.

Brabant, C., Alleva, L., Quertemont, E., and Tirelli, E. (2010 Nov). Involvement of the brain histaminergic system in addiction and addiction-related behaviors: A comprehensive review with emphasis on the potential therapeutic use of histaminergic compounds in drug dependence. *Prog Neurobiol,* 92(3), 421–41.

Breslau, N., Davis, G. C., Andreski, P., and Peterson, E. (1991 Mar). Traumatic events and post-traumatic stress disorder in an urban population of young adults. *Arch Gen Psychiatry,* 48(3), 216–22.

Bricker, G. V. (2014 Oct). Isothiocyanate metabolism, distribution, and interconversion in mice following consumption of thermally processed broccoli sprouts or purified sulforaphane. *Mol Nutr Food Res,* 58(10), 1991–2000.

Brown, N. W. (2008). *Children of the Self-Absorbed* (2nd ed.). Oakland, CA: New Harbinger Publications, Inc.

Bruhn, C. (2014). The reward system of the brain: The brain loves surprises. *Dtsch Med Wochenschr,* 139(18), 928–9.

Cable, N., Bartley, M., Chandola, T., and Sacker, A. (2013). Friends are equally important to men and women, but family matters more for men's well-being. *J Epidemiol Community Health,* 67(2), 166–71.

Casement, M. D., Shaw, D. S., Sitnick, S. L., Musselman, S. C., and Forbes, E. E. (2014 May 1). Life stress in adolescence predicts early adult reward-related brain function and alcohol dependence. *Soc Cogn Affect Neurosci.* Retrieved from www.ncbi.nlm.nih.gov/pubmed/24795442

Cheren, M., Foushi, M., Gudmundsdotter, E. H., Hillock, C., Lerner, M., Prager, M., Rice, M., Walsh, L., and Werdell, P. (2009). Physical craving and food addiction. *The Food Addiction Institute.* Retrieved from http://foodaddiction institute.org/scientific-research/physical-craving-and-food-addiction-a -scientific-review

Clay, R. A. (2011 Jan). Stressed in America. *American Psychological Association,* 42(1), 60.

Clement, A. M., and Clement, B. R. (2011). *Killer Clothes.* Summertown, TN: Hippocrates Publications.

Colantuoni, C., Rada, P., McCarthy, J., Patten, C., Avena, N. M., Chadeayne, A., and Hoebel, B. G. (2002). Evidence that intermittent, excessive sugar intake causes endogenous opioid dependence. *Obesity Research,* 10, 478–88.

Collinge W., Kahn J., and Soltysik R. (2012 Dec). Promoting reintegration of National Guard veterans and their partners using a self-directed program of integrative therapies: A pilot study. *Mil Med,* 177(12), 1477–85.

Currier, J. M., Holland, J. M., and Drescher, K. D. (2015 Jan 26). Spirituality factors in the prediction of outcomes of PTSD treatment for U.S. military veterans. *Journal of Traumatic Stress.* doi: 10.1002/jts.21978

Davidson, J. R., Hughes, D., Blazer, D. G., and George, L. K. (1991 Aug). Posttraumatic stress disorder in the community: An epidemiological study. *Psychol Med,* 21(3), 713–21.

Delisle, I. (1998 Nov). Solitude. *The Canadian Nurse,* 94(10), 40–1, 44.

Dietz, T. J., Davis, D., and Pennings, J. (2012). Evaluating animal-assisted therapy in group treatment for child sexual abuse. *J Child Sex Abus,* 21(6), 665–83.

DiMauro, J., Carter, S., Folk, J. B., and Kashdan, T. B. (2014 Dec). A historical review of trauma-related diagnoses to reconsider the heterogeneity of PTSD. *J Anxiety Disord,* 28(8), 774–86.

Eikenaes, I., Hummelen, B., Abrahamsen, G., Andrea, H., and Wilberg, T. (2013 Dec). Personality functioning in patients with avoidant personality disorder and social phobia. *J Pers Disord,* 27(6), 746–63.

England, D. (2009). *The Post-traumatic Stress Disorder Relationship.* Avon, MA: Adams Media.

Environmental Protection Agency (U.S.). (2009). Toxicological Review of Tetrachloroethylene (Perchloroethylene).

———. (January 2015). Fact Sheet on Perchloroethylene, also known as Tetrachloroethylene.

Epel, E. S., McEwen, B., Seeman, T., Matthews, K., Castellazzo, G., Brownell, K. D., Bell, J., and Ickovics, J. R. (2000). Stress and body shape: Stress-induced cortisol secretion is consistently greater among women with central fat. *Psychosomatic Medicine,* 62(5), 623–32.

Eutamene, H., Theodorou, V., Fioramonti, J., and Bueno, L. (2003 Dec 15). Acute stress modulates the histamine content of mast cells in the gastrointestinal tract through interleukin-1 and corticotropin-releasing factor release in rats. *J Physiol,* 553(Pt 3), 959–66.

Ezemonye, L., and Ikpesu, T. O. (2011 Sep). Evaluation of sub-lethal effects of endosulfan on cortisol secretion, glutathione S-transferase and acetylcholinesterase activities in Clarias gariepinus. *Food Chem Toxicol,* 49(9), 1898–903.

Fava, M., Alpert, J., Nierenberg, A. A., Mischoulon, D., Otto, M. W., Zajecka, J., Murck, H., and Rosenbaum, J. F. (2005 Oct). A double-blind, randomized trial of St John's wort, fluoxetine, and placebo in major depressive disorder. *J Clin Psychopharmacol,* 25(5), 441–7.

Ferguson, P. E., Persinger, D., and Steele, M. (2010 Mar 17). Resolving dilemmas through bodywork. *Int J Ther Massage Bodywork,* 3(1), 41–7.

Field, T. (2002 Jan). Massage therapy. *Med Clin North Am,* 86(1), 163–71.

Field, T., Hernandez-Reif, M., Diego, M., Schanberg, S., and Kuhn, C. (2005 Oct). Cortisol decreases and serotonin and dopamine increase following massage therapy. *Int J Neurosci,* 115(10), 1397–413.

Finkelhor, D., Ormrod, R. K., and Turner, H. A. (2007 May). Re-victimization patterns in a national longitudinal sample of children and youth. *Child Abuse and Neglect,* 31(5), 479–502.

Friedman, L. C., Nelson, D. V., Baer, P. E., Lane, M., Smith, F. E., and Dworkin R. J. (1992 April). The relationship of dispositional optimism, daily life stress, and domestic environment to coping methods used by cancer patients. *Journal of Behavioral Medicine,* 15(2), 127–41.

Fu, W., Sood, S., and Hedges, D. W. (2010). Hippocampal volume deficits associated with exposure to psychological trauma and posttraumatic stress disorder in adults: A meta-analysis. *Progress in Neuro-Psychopharmacology and Biological Psychiatry,* 34(7), 1181–8.

Fujimaki, H., Kawagoe A., Bissonnette, E., and Befus, D. (1992). Mast cell response to formaldehyde. 1. Modulation of mediator release. *Int Arch Allergy Immunol,* 98(4), 324–31.

Gangi, S., and Johansson, O. (2000 Apr). A theoretical model based upon mast cells and histamine to explain the recently proclaimed sensitivity to electric and/or magnetic fields in humans. *Med Hypotheses,* 54(4), 663–71.

Garcia-Segura, L. M. (2009). *Hormones and Brain Plasticity.* New York: Oxford University Press.

Gilbertson, M. W., Shenton, M. E., Ciszewski, A., Kasai, K. Lasko, N. B., Orr, S. P., and Pitman, R. K. (2002 Nov). Smaller hippocampal volume predicts pathologic vulnerability to psychological trauma. *Nat Neurosci,* 5(11), 1242–7.

Goel, N., Kim, H., and Lao, R. P. (2005). An olfactory stimulus modifies nighttime sleep in young men and women. *Chronobiol Int,* 22(5), 889–904.

Gopal, A., Mondal, S., Gandhi, A., Arora, S., and Bhattacharjee, J. (2011 Jan–June). Effect of integrated yoga practices on immune responses in examination stress: A preliminary study. *Int J Yoga,* 4(1), 26–32.

Graevskaya, E. (2003 Jan). Effect of methylmercury on histamine release from rat mast cells. *Archives of Toxicology,* 77(1), 17–21

Grinage, B. D. (2003 Dec 15). Diagnosis and management of post-traumatic stress disorder. *Am Fam Physician,* 68(12), 2401–8.

Grosso, J. A, Kimbrel, N. A, Dolan, S., Meyer, E. C., Kruse, M. I., Gulliver, S. B., and Morissette, S. B. (2014 Aug). A test of whether coping styles moderate the effect of PTSD symptoms on alcohol outcomes. *Journal of Traumatic Stress,* 27(4), 478–82.

Guarneri-White, M. E., Jensen-Campbell, L. A., and Knack, J. M. (2015 Feb). Is co-ruminating with friends related to health problems in victimized adolescents? *J Adolesc,* 39, 15–26.

Hagel, A. F., Layritz, C. M., Hagel, W. H., Hagel, H. J., Hagel, E., Dauth, W., Kressel, J., Regnet, T., Rosenberg, A., Neurath, M. F., Molderings, G. J., and Raithel, M. (2013 Sep). Intravenous infusion of ascorbic acid decreases serum histamine concentrations in patients with allergic and non-allergic diseases. *Naunyn Schmiedebergs Arch Pharmacol,* 386(9), 789–93.

Harvey, A. G., Jones, C., and Schmidt, D. A. (2003 May). Sleep and posttraumatic stress disorder: A review. *Clinical Psychology Review,* 23(3), 377–407.

He, F., Cao, R., Feng, Z., Guan, H., and Peng, J. (2013 Dec 17). The impacts of dispositional optimism and psychological resilience on the subjective well-being of burn patients: A structural equation modelling analysis. *PLoS One,* 8(12), e82939.

Hidalgo, R. B., and Davidson, J. (2000). Posttraumatic stress disorder: Epidemiology and health-related considerations. *J Clin Pychiatry,* 61(suppl 7), 5–13.

Hodge, L., Yan, K. Y., and Loblay, R. L. (1996 Aug). Assessment of food chemical intolerance in adult asthmatic subjects.. *Thorax,* 51(8), 805–9.

Hölzel, B. K., Carmody, J., Evans, K. C., Hoge, E. A., Dusek, J. A., Morgan, L., and Lazar, S. W. (2010 Mar). Stress reduction correlates with structural changes in the amygdala. *Soc Cogn Affect Neurosci,* 5(1), 11–17.

Hosseinbor, M., Ardekani, S. M., Bakhshani, S., and Bakhshani, S. (2014 Aug 25). Emotional and social loneliness in individuals with and without substance dependence disorder. *Int J High Risk Behav Addict,* 3(3), e22688.

Hou, W. H., Chiang, P. T., Hsu, T. Y., Chiu, S. Y., and Yen, Y. C. (2010). Treatment effects of massage therapy in depressed people: A meta-analysis. *J Clin Psychiatry.* 71(7), 894–901.

Huang, Z. L., Mochizuki, T., Watanabe, H., and Maeyama, K. (1999 Aug 6). Activation of sensory nerves participates in stress-induced histamine release from mast cells in rats. *Neurosci Lett,* 270(3), 181–4.

Huszti, Z., and Balogh, I. (1995 Jun). Effects of lead and mercury on histamine uptake by glial and endothelial cells. *Pharmacol Toxicol,* 76(6), 339–42.

Huxhold, O., Miche, M., and Schüz, B. (2014 May). Benefits of having friends in older ages: Differential effects of informal social activities on well-being in middle-aged and older adults. *J Gerontol B Psychol Sci Soc Sci.* 69(3), 366–75.

Iribarren, J., Prolo, P., Neagos, N., and Chiappelli, F. (2005 Dec). Post-traumatic stress disorder: Evidence-based research for the third millennium. *Evid Based Complement Alternat Med,* 2(4), 503–512.

Itai, T., Amayasu, H., Kuribayashi, M., Kawamura, N., Okada, M., Momose, A., Tateyama, T., Narumi, K., Uematsu, W., and Kaneko, S. (2000 Aug). Psychological effects of aromatherapy on chronic hemodialysis patients. *Psychiatry Clin Neurosci,* 54(4), 393–7.

Jan, J. E., Espezel, H., and Appleton, R. E. (1994 Feb). The treatment of sleep disorders with melatonin. *Developmental Medicine and Child Neurology,* 36(2), 97–107.

Jarisch, R., Weyer, D., Ehlert, E., Koch, C. H., Pinkowski, E., Jung, P., Kähler, W., Girgensohn, R., Kowalski, J., Weisser, B., and Koch, A. (2014). Impact of oral vitamin C on histamine levels and seasickness. *J Vestib Res,* 24(4), 281–8.

Johansson, O., Gangi, S., Liang, Y., Yoshimura, K., Jing, C., and Liu, P.-Y. (2001 Nov). Cutaneous mast cells are altered in normal healthy volunteers sitting in front of ordinary TVs/PCs--results from open-field provocation experiments. *J Cutan Pathol,* 28(10), 513–9.

Jovanovic, T., Norrholm, S. D., Blanding, N. Q., Davis, M., Duncan, E., Bradley, B., and Ressler, K. J. (2010 Mar). Impaired fear inhibition is a biomarker of PTSD but not depression. *Depress Anxiety,* 27(3), 244–51.

Kamei, T., Toriumi, Y., Kimura, H., Ohno, S., Kumano, H., and Kimura, K. (2000 Jun). Decrease in serum cortisol during yoga exercise is correlated with alpha wave activation. *Percept Mot Skills,* 90(3 Pt 1), 1027–32.

Kanojia, S., Sharma, V. K., Gandhi, A., Kapoor, R., Kukreja, A., and Subramanian, S. K. (2013 Oct). Effect of yoga on autonomic functions and psychological status during both phases of menstrual cycle in young healthy females. *J Clin Diagn Res,* 7(10), 2133–9.

Kashdan, T. B., Uswatte, G., and Julian, T. (2006 Feb). Gratitude and hedonic and eudaimonic well-being in Vietnam war veterans. *Behav Res Ther,* 44(2), 177–99.

Kasper, S., Gastpar, M., Müller, W. E., Volz, H. P., Dienel, A., Kieser, M., and Möller, H. J. (2008 Feb). Efficacy of St. John's wort extract WS 5570 in acute treatment of mild depression: A reanalysis of data from controlled clinical trials. *Eur Arch Psychiatry Clin Neurosci,* 258(1), 59–63.

Kather, H., and Simon, B. (1979 Oct 27). Opioid peptides and obesity. *Lancet,* 314(8148), 905.

Kempton, M. J., Salvador, Z., Munafò, M. R., Geddes, J. R., Simmons, A., Frangou, S., and Williams, S. C. (2011 Jul). Structural neuroimaging studies in major depressive disorder: Meta-analysis and comparison with bipolar disorder. *Arch Gen Psychiatry,* 68(7), 675–90.

Khalfa, S., Bella, S. D., Roy, M., Peretz, I., and Lupien, S. J. (2003). Effects of relaxing music on salivary cortisol level after psychological stress. *Ann NY Acad Sci,* 999: 374–6.

Khanam, A. A., Sachdeva, U., Guleria, R., and Deepak, K. K. (1996 Oct). Study of pulmonary and autonomic functions of asthma patients after yoga training. *Indian J Physiol Pharmacol,* 40(4), 318–24.

Kiecolt-Glaser, J., and Glaser, R. (2008 Aug 14). Stress, anxiety can make allergy attacks even more miserable and last longer. Presentation at the American Psychological Association Annual Meeting in Boston, MA.

Komori, T., Fujiwara, R., Tanida, M., Nomura, J., and Yokoyama, M. M. (1995 May–Jun). Effects of citrus fragrance on immune function and depressive states. *Neuroimmunomodulation,* 2(3), 174–80.

Kostek, J. A., Beck, K. D, Gilbertson, M. W., Orr, S. P., Pang, K. C., Servatius, R. J., and Myers, C. E. (2014 Dec). Acquired equivalence in U.S. veterans with symptoms of posttraumatic stress: Reexperiencing symptoms are associated with greater generalization. *Journal of Traumatic Stress,* 27(6), 717–20.

Kreutz, G., Bongard, S., Rohrmann, S., Hodapp, V., and Grebe, D. (2004 Dec). Effects of choir singing or listening on secretory immunoglobulin A, cortisol, and emotional state. *J Behav Med,* 27(6), 623–35.

Kristal, A. R., Littman, A. J., Benitez, D., and White, E. (2005). Yoga practice is associated with attenuated weight gain in healthy, middle-aged men and women. *Altern Ther Health Med,* 11(4), 28–33.

Kubany, E. S., Haynes, S. N., Leisen, M. B., Owens, J. A., Kaplan, A. S., Watson, S. B., and Burns, K. (2000 Jun). Development and preliminary validation of a brief broad-spectrum measure of trauma exposure: The traumatic life events questionnaire. *Psychol Assess,* 12(2), 210–24.

Kuijer, R. G., and Boyce, J. A. (2012 Jun). Emotional eating and its effect on eating behaviour after a natural disaster. *Appetite,* 58(3), 936–39.

Laakmann, G., Schüle, C., Baghai, T., and Kieser, M. (1998 Jun). St. John's wort in mild to moderate depression: The relevance of hyperforin for the clinical efficacy. *Pharmacopsychiatry,* 31(Suppl 1), 54–9.

Landau, D. (2011 Mar). Stressful life events and material deprivation in hoarding disorder. *J Anxiety Disord,* 25(2), 192–202.

Lane, J. D. (March 2011). Caffeine, glucose metabolism, and type 2 diabetes. *Journal of Caffeine Research,* 1(1), 23–28.

Lanius, R., Miller, M., Wolf, E., Brand, B., Frewen, P., Vermetten, E., and Spiegel, D. (2014 Jan 3). Dissociative subtype of PTSD. *PTSD: National Center for PTSD, U.S. Department of Veterans Affairs.* Retrieved from www.ptsd.va.gov/professional/PTSD-overview/Dissociative_Subtype_of_PTSD.asp

Larson, R. W. (1997 Feb). The emergence of solitude as a constructive domain of experience in early adolescence. *Child Dev.* 68(1), 80–93.

Lazar, S. W., Bush, G., Gollub, R. L., Fricchione, G. L., Khalsa, G., and Benson, H. (2000 May 15). Functional brain mapping of the relaxation response and meditation. *Neuroreport,* 11(7), 1581–5.

Leary, M. R., and Springer, C.A. (2000). Hurt feelings: The neglected emotion. In R. M. Kowalski (Ed.), *Behaving Badly: Aversive Behaviors in Interpersonal Relationships.* Washington, D.C.: American Psychological Association.

Levine, P. A. (2010). *In an Unspoken Voice: How the Body Releases Trauma and Restores Goodness.* Berkeley, CA: North Atlantic Books.

Lillehei, A. S., and Halcon, L. L. (2014 Jun). A systematic review of the effect of inhaled essential oils on sleep. *J Altern Complement Med,* 20(6), 441–51.

Long, B., and Haney, C. (1988 Dec). Long-term follow-up of stressed working women: A comparison of aerobic exercise and progressive relaxation. *Journal of Sport and Exercise Psychology*, 10(4), 461–70.

Lovallo, W. R., Whitsett, T., al'Absi, M., Sung, B. H., Vincent, A. S., and Wilson, M. F. (2005). Caffeine stimulation of cortisol secretion across the waking hours in relation to caffeine intake levels. *Psychosom Med*, 67(5), 734–9.

Maintz, L., and Novak, L. (2007). Histamine and histamine intolerance. *Am J Clin Nutri*, 85(5), 1185–96.

Maršanić, V. B., Aukst, M. B., Jukić, V., Matko, V., and Grgić, V. (2014 May). Self-reported emotional and behavioral symptoms, parent-adolescent bonding and family functioning in clinically referred adolescent offspring of Croatian PTSD war veterans. *Eur Child Adolesc Psychiatry*, 23(5), 295–306.

Mayo Clinic Staff. (2014 Apr 8). Relaxation techniques. *Mayo Clinic*. Retrieved from www.mayoclinic.org/healthy-living/stress-management/basics/relaxation-techniques/hlv-20049495

McCraty, R., Barrios-Choplin, B., Atkinson, M., and Tomasino, D. (1998 Jan). The effects of different types of music on mood, tension, and mental clarity. *Altern Ther Health Med*, 4(1), 75–84.

McKay, D. L., and Blumberg, J. B. (2006 Jul). A review of the bioactivity and potential health benefits of chamomile tea (Matricaria recutita L.). *Phytother Res*, 20(7), 519–30.

McPherson, F., and Schwenka, M. A. (2004). Use of complementary and alternative therapies among active duty soldiers, military retirees, and family members at a military hospital. *Mil Med*, 169(5), 354–7.

Mealer, M., Burnham, E. L., Goode, C. J., Rothbaum, B., and Moss, M. (2009). The prevalence and impact of post traumatic stress disorder and burnout syndrome in nurses. *Depression and Anxiety*, 26(12), 1118–26.

Meewisse, M. L., Reitsma, J. B., de Vries, G. J., Gersons, B. P., and Olff, M. (2007 Nov). Cortisol and post-traumatic stress disorder in adults: Systematic review and meta-analysis. *The British Journal of Psychiatry*, 191, 387–92.

Melzer, D., Rice, N. E., Lewis, C., Henley, W. E., and Galloway, T. S. (2010 Jan 13). Association of urinary bisphenol A concentration with heart disease: Evidence from NHANES 2003/06. *PLoS One*, 5(1), e8673.

Mitchell, K. S., Dick, A. M., DiMartino, D. M., Smith, B. N., Niles, B., Koenen, K. C., and Street, A. (2014 Apr). A pilot study of a randomized controlled trial of yoga as an intervention for PTSD symptoms in women. *Journal of Traumatic Stress*, 27(2), 121–8.

Moon, M. K., Jeong, I. K., Oh, T. J., Ahn, H. Y., Kim, H. H., Park,Y. J., Jang, H. C., and Park, K. S. (2015 May 13). Long-term oral exposure to bisphenol A induces glucose intolerance and insulin resistance. *J Endocrinol*, pii: JOE-14-0714.

Morin, C. M., Koetter, U., Bastien, C., Ware, J. C., and Wooten, V. (2005 Nov). Valerian-hops combination and diphenhydramine for treating insomnia: A randomized placebo-controlled clinical trial. *Sleep*, 28(11), 1465–71.

Morris, M. J., and Pavia, M. M. (2004 Apr 23). Increased endogenous noradrenaline and neuropeptide Y release from the hypothalamus of streptozotocin diabetic rats. *Brain Res*, 1006(1), 100–6.

Moyer, C. A., Rounds, J., and Hannum, J. W. (2004). A meta-analysis of massage therapy research. *Psychol Bulletin*, 130(1), 3–18.

Mubarak, A., Hodgson, J. M., Considine, M. J., Croft, K. D., and Matthews, V. B. (2013). Supplementation of a high-fat diet with chlorogenic acid is associated with insulin resistance and hepatic lipid accumulation in mice. *J Agric Food Chem*, 61(18), 4371–8.

Nakajima, Y., Goldblum, R. M., and Midoro-Horiuti, T. (2012). Fetal exposure to bisphenol A as a risk factor for the development of childhood asthma: An animal model study. *Environ Health*, 11, 1–7.

Nauert, R. (2013 May 2). Child abuse, later PTSD show distinctive genetic signature. *Psych Central*. Retrieved from http://psychcentral.com/news/2013/05/02/child-abuse-later-ptsd-show-distinctive-genetic-signature/54377.html

Newball, H. H., Donlon, M. A., Procell, L. R., Helgeson, E. A., and Franz, D. R. (1986 Sep). Organophosphate-induced histamine release from mast cells. *Pharmacol Exp Ther*, 238(3), 839–45.

Newmeyer, M., Keyes, B., Gregory, S., Palmer, K., Buford, D., Mondt, P., and Okai, B. (2014 Autumn). The Mother Teresa effect: The modulation of spirituality in using the CISM model with mental health service providers. *Int J Emerg Ment Health*, 16(1), 251–8.

O'Brien, E., Dolinoy, D. C., and Mancuso, P. (2014 Jan–Mar). Bisphenol A at concentrations relevant to human exposure enhances histamine and cysteinyl leukotriene release from bone marrow-derived mast cells. *J Immunotoxicol*, 11(1), 84 9.

Oken, B. S., Zajdel, D., Kishiyama, S., Flegal, K., Dehen, C., Haas, M., Kraemer, D., Lawrence, J., and Leyva, J. (2006). Randomized, controlled, six-month trial of yoga in healthy seniors: Effects on cognition and quality of life. *Alternative Therapies in Health and Medicine*, 12(1), 40–7.

Olff, M. (2012). Bonding after trauma: On the role of social support and the oxytocin system in traumatic stress. *Eur J Psychotraumatol*, 3, 10.3402. doi: 10.3402/ejpt.v3i0.18597

Omini, C., Hernandez, A., Zuccari, G., Clavenna, G., Daffonchio, L. (1990). Passive cigarette smoke exposure induces airway hyperreactivity to histamine but not to acetylcholine in guinea-pigs. *Pulm Pharmacol*, 3(3), 145–50.

Parrott, R. F., Heavens, R. P., and Baldwin, B. A. (1986). Stimulation of feeding in the satiated pig by intracerebroventricular injection of neuropeptide Y. *Physiol. Behav*, 36(3), 523–5.

Perry, R., Terry, R., Watson, L. K., and Ernst, E. (2012 Jun 15). Is lavender an anxiolytic drug? A systematic review of randomized clinical trials. *Phytomedicine*, 19(8–9), 825–35.

Pineles, S. L. (2011 Feb). Trauma reactivity, avoidant coping, and PTSD symptoms: a moderating relationship? *J Abnorm Psychol*, 120(1), 240–6.

Pittler, M. H., and Ernst, E. (2000 Feb). Efficacy of kava extract for treating anxiety: Systematic review and meta-analysis. *J Clin Psychopharmacol*, 20(1), 84–9.

Polheber, J. P., and Matchock, R. L. (2014 Oct). The presence of a dog attenuates cortisol and heart rate in the Trier Social Stress Test compared to human friends. *J Behav Med*, 37(5), 860–7.

Potter, P., Deshields, T., and Rodriguez, S. (2013 Oct–Dec). Developing a systemic program for compassion fatigue. *Nurse Administration Quarterly*, 37(4), 326–32.

Prasad, A., Zuzek, R. W., Weinsier, S. B., Latif, S. R., Linsky, R. A., Ahmed, H. N., and Sadiq, I. (2009 Apr 1). Clinical characteristics and four-year outcomes of patients in the Rhode Island Takotsubo Cardiomyopathy Registry. *American Journal of Cardiology*, 103(7), 1015–19.

Price, J. L. (2014 Jan 3). When a child's parent has PTSD. *US Department of Veteran's Affairs*. Retrieved from www.ptsd.va.gov/professional/treatment/children/pro_child_parent_ptsd.asp

Puleo, G. (2014). Burnout and post-traumatic stress disorder. TedX Talk at Seton Hill University in Greensburg, PA. Retrieved from http://tedxtalks.ted.com/video/Burnout-and-post-traumatic-stre

Rajkovic, V. (2005 Jul). Histological characteristics of cutaneous and thyroid mast cell populations in male rats exposed to power-frequency electromagnetic fields. *Int J Radiat Biol*, 81(7), 491–9.

Raub, J. A. (2002). Psychophysiologic effects of hatha yoga on musculoskeletal and cardiopulmonary function: A literature review. *The Journal of Alternative and Complementary Medicine*, 8(6), 797–812.

Rioux, J. G., and Ritenbaugh, C. (2013 May–Jun). Narrative review of yoga intervention clinical trials including weight-related outcomes. *Altern Ther Health Med*, 19(3), 32–46.

Rohr, U., König, W., and Selenka, F. (1985 Dec). Effect of pesticides on the release of histamine, chemotactic factors and leukotrienes from rat mast cells and human basophils. *Zentrabl Bakteriol Mikrobiol Hyg B*, 181(6), 469–86.

Ross, A., and Thomas, S. (2010). The health benefits of yoga and exercise: A review of comparison studies. *Journal of Alternative and Complementary Medicine*, 16(1), 3–12.

Roth, S., and Cohen, L. (1986). Approach, avoidance, and coping with stress. *American Psychologist*, 41(7), 813–9.

Sakamoto, T., Kamijimab, M., and Miyakec, M. (2012 Jun 15). Neurogenic airway microvascular leakage induced by toluene inhalation in rats. *Eur J Pharmacol.* 685(1–3), 180–5.

Sansone, R. A., and Sansone, L. A. (2010 Nov). Gratitude and well being: The benefits of appreciation. *Psychiatry (Edgmont),* 7(11), 18–22.

Sapolsky, R. M. (2004). *Why zebras don't get ulcers* (3rd ed.). New York: St. Martin's Griffin.

Sarris, J., Kavanagh, D. J., Byrne, G., Bone, K. M., Adams, J., and Deed, G. (2009 Aug). The Kava Anxiety Depression Spectrum Study (KADSS): A randomized, placebo-controlled crossover trial using an aqueous extract of Piper methysticum. *Psychopharmacology (Berl),* 205(3), 399–407.

Sarris, J., LaPorte, E., and Schweitzer, I. (2011). Kava: A comprehensive review of efficacy, safety, and psychopharmacology. *Aust N Z J Psychiatry,* 45(1), 27–35.

Sato, T. (1998 Feb 20). Augmentation of allergic reactions by several pesticides. *Toxicology.* 126(1), 41–53.

Schaubschläger, W. W., Becker, W. M., Schade, U., Zabel, P., and Schlaak, M. (1991). Release of mediators from human gastric mucosa and blood in adverse reactions to benzoate. *Int Arch Allergy Appl Immunol,* 96(2), 97–101.

Schnyder, U., and Cloitre, M., Eds. (2015). *Evidence-based treatments for trauma-related psychological disorders: A practical guide for clinicians.* New York: Springer.

Seo, M. (2008). A small amount of tetrachloroethylene ingestion from drinking water accelerates antigen-stimulated allergic responses. *Immunobiology,* 213(8), 663–9.

Seppälä, E. M., Nitschke, J. B., Tudorascu, D. L., Hayes, A., Goldstein, M. R., Nguyen, D. T., Perlman, D., and Davidson, R. J. (2014 Aug). Breathing-based meditation decreases posttraumatic stress disorder symptoms in U.S. military veterans: A randomized controlled longitudinal study. *Journal of Traumatic Stress,* 27(4), 397–405.

Sherman, K. J., Cherkin, D. C., Wellman, R. D., Cook, A. J., Hawkes, R. J., Delaney, K., and Deyo, R. A. (2011 Dec 12). A randomized trial comparing yoga, stretching, and a self-care book for chronic low back pain. *Archives of Internal Medicine,* 171(22), 2019–26.

Sijbrandij, M., Engelhard, I. M., Lommen, M. J., Leer, A., and Baas, J. M. (2013 Dec). Impaired fear inhibition learning predicts the persistence of symptoms of posttraumatic stress disorder (PTSD). *Journal of Psychiatric Research,* 47(12), 1991–7.

Sleiman, M., Gundel, L. A., Pankow, J. F., Jacob, P., Singer, B. C., and Destaillats, H. (April 2010). Formation of carcinogens indoors by surface-mediated reactions of nicotine with nitrous acid, leading to potential thirdhand smoke hazards. *Proc Natl Acad Sci,* 107(15), 6576–81.

Smith, C., Klosterbuer, A., and Levine, A. S. (2009 Apr). Military experience strongly influences post-service eating behavior and BMI status in American veterans. *Appetite,* 52(2), 280–9.

Srivastava, J. K., Shankar, E., and Gupta, S. (2010). Chamomile: A herbal medicine of the past with bright future. *Molecular Medicine Reports,* 3(6), 895–901.

Steinemann, A. C., Gallagher, L. G., Davis, A. L., MacGregor, I. C. (2011). Chemical emissions from residential dryer vents during use of fragranced laundry products. *Air Qual Atmos Health,* 6(1), 151–6.

Stevinson, C., and Ernst, E. (2000 Apr 1). Valerian for insomnia: A systematic review of randomized clinical trials. *Sleep Med,* 1(2), 91–9.

Stewart, S. H. (1996 Jul). Alcohol abuse in individuals exposed to trauma: A critical review. *Psychological Bulletin,* 120(1), 83–112.

Tanaka, Y., Nakase, Y., Yamaguchi, M., Sugimoto, N., Ohara, K., Nagase, H., and Ohta, K. (2014). Allergy to formaldehyde, basophil histamine-release test is useful for diagnosis. *Int Arch Allergy Immunol,* 164(1), 27–9.

Thakkar, M. M. (2001 Feb). Histamine in the regulation of wakefulness. *Sleep Med Rev,* 15(1), 65–74.

Theoharides, T. C., and Cochrane, D. E. (2004 Jan). Critical role of mast cells in inflammatory diseases and the effect of acute stress. *Journal of Neuroimmunology,* 146(1–2), 1–12.

Tilbrook, H. E., Cox, H., Hewitt, C. E., Kang'ombe, A. R., Chuang, L. H., Jayakody, S., Aplin, J. D., Semlyen, A., Trewhela, A., Watt, I., and Torgerson, D. J. (2011 Nov 1). Yoga for chronic low back pain: A randomized trial. *Annals of Internal Medicine,* 155(9), 569–78.

Tomiyama, J. A. (2014 Nov 1). Weight stigma is stressful: A review of evidence for the Cyclic Obesity/Weight-Based Stigma model. *Appetite,* 82, 8–15.

Trappe, H. J. (2010 Dec). The effects of music on the cardiovascular system and cardiovascular health. *Heart,* 96(23), 1868–71.

Uebelacker, L. A., Epstein-Lubow, G., Gaudiano, B. A., Tremont, G., Battle, C. L., and Miller, I. W. (2010 Jan 16). Hatha yoga for depression: A critical review of the evidence for efficacy, plausible mechanisms of action, and directions for future research. *Journal of Psychiatric Practice,* 16(1), 22–33.

United States Department of Agriculture. National nutrient database for standard reference, release 27. *The National Agricultural Library.* Retrieved from http://ndb.nal.usda.gov/ndb/search/list

University of Michigan Health System. (2011 Feb 8). New link between genes and stress response, depression: Neuropeptide Y. *Science Daily.* Retrieved from www.sciencedaily.com/releases/2011/02/110207165426.htm.

van der Kolk, B. A. (2011). Introduction. In D. Emerson and E. Hopper, Eds., *Overcoming Trauma Through Yoga: Reclaiming Your Body.* Berkeley, CA: North Atlantic Books.

van der Kolk, B. A. (2014). *The Body Keeps the Score: Brain, Mind, and Body in the Healing of Trauma*. New York: Viking.

VanderEnde, D. S., and Morrow, J. D. (2001 Jul). Release of markedly increased quantities of prostaglandin D2 from the skin in vivo in humans after the application of cinnamic aldehyde. *J Am Acad Dermatol*, 45(1), 62–7.

Vilhena, E., Pais-Ribeiro, J., Silva, I., Pedro, L., Meneses, R. F., Cardoso, H., Silva, A. M., and Mendonça, D. (2014 Jul). Optimism on quality of life in Portuguese chronic patients: Moderator/mediator? *Rev Assoc Med Br*, 60(4), 373–80.

Vilijaa, M., and Romualdas, M. (2014 Mar). Unhealthy food in relation to posttraumatic stress symptoms among adolescents. *Appetite*, 74, 86–91.

Vrbanac, Z., Zecević, I., Ljubić, M., Belić, M., Stanin, D., Bottegaro, N. B., Jurkić, G., Skrlin, B., Bedrica, L., and Zubcić, D. (2013 Sep). Animal assisted therapy and perception of loneliness in geriatric nursing home residents. *Coll Antropol*, 37(3), 973–6.

Walker, P. (2013). *Complex PTSD: From Surviving to Thriving*. Lafayette, CA: Azure Coyote Publishing, printed by CreateSpace.

Wardle, J. (1987 Feb). Compulsive eating and dietary restraint. *British Journal of Clinical Psychology*, 26(1), 47–55.

Wegner, M., Schüler, J., and Budde, H. (2014 Oct). The implicit affiliation motive moderates cortisol responses to acute psychosocial stress in high school students. *Psychoneuroendocrinology*, 48, 162–8.

West, D. J. (1960). Visionary and hallucinatory experiences: A comparative appraisal. *International Journal of Parapsychology*, 2(1), 89–100.

Westphal, V. K., and Smith, J. E. (1996). Overeaters Anonymous: Who goes and who succeeds? *International Journal of Eating Disorders*, 4, 160–70.

Wilson, G. T., and Fairburn, C. G. (1998). Treatments for eating disorders. In P. E. Nathan and J. M. Gorman, Eds., *A Guide to Treatments That Work*. New York: Oxford University Press.

Wilson, S. A., Becker, L. A., and Tinker, R. H. (1997 Dec). Fifteen-month follow-up of eye movement desensitization and reprocessing (EMDR) treatment for posttraumatic stress disorder and psychological trauma. *J Consult Clin Psychol*, 65(6), 1047–56.

Wingenfeld, K., and Wolf, O. (2015 Jan). Effects of cortisol on cognition in major depressive disorder, posttraumatic stress disorder and borderline personality disorder—2014 Curt Richter Award Winner. *Psychoneuroendocrinology*, 51, 282–95.

Wirth, M. M., and Schultheiss, O. C. (2006 Dec). Effects of affiliation arousal (hope of closeness) and affiliation stress (fear of rejection) on progesterone and cortisol. *Horm Behav*, 50(5), 786–95.

Wolf, L. D., Davis, M. C., Yeung, E. W., and Tennen, H. A. (2015 Jan 8). The within-day relation between lonely episodes and subsequent clinical pain in individuals with fibromyalgia: Mediating role of pain cognitions. *Journal of Psychosomatic Research.* Retrieved from http://dx.doi.org/10.1016/j.jpsychores .2014.12.018.

Woodyard, C. (2011 Jul–Dec). Exploring the therapeutic effects of yoga and its ability to increase quality of life. *Int J Yoga,* 4(2): 49–54.

Wortmann, J. H., Park, C. L., and Edmondson, D. (2011). Trauma and PTSD symptoms: Does spiritual struggle mediate the link? *Psychol Trauma,* 3(4), 442–52.

Ye, Y., and Lin, L. (2015 Jan 26). Examining relations between locus of control, loneliness, subjective well-being, and preference for online social interaction. *Psychological Reports.* doi: 10.2466/07.09.PR0.116k14w3.

Yeung, E. W., Davis, M. C., Aiken, L. S., and Tennen, H. A. (2014 Nov 8). Daily social enjoyment interrupts the cycle of same-day and next-day fatigue in women with fibromyalgia. *Ann Behav Med.* Retrieved from www.ncbi.nlm .nih.gov/pubmed/25380634.

Yuen, K. W., Garner, J. P., Carson, D. S., Keller, J., Lembke, A., Hyde, S. A., and Parker, K. J. (2014 Apr). Plasma oxytocin concentrations are lower in depressed vs. healthy control women and are independent of cortisol. *Journal of Psychiatric Research,* 51, 30–6.

Zampeli, E., and Tiligada, E. (2009 May). The role of histamine H4 receptor in immune and inflammatory disorders. *British Journal of Pharmacology,* 157(1), 24–33.

Zioudrou, C., Streaty, R. A., and Klee, W. A. (1979 Apr 10). Opioid peptides derived from food proteins: The exorphins. *Journal of Biological Chemistry,* 254(7), 2446–9.

Index

About the Author

Doreen Virtue holds B.A., M.A., and Ph.D. degrees in counseling psychology. A former psychotherapist specializing in eating disorders and addictions, Doreen now gives online workshops on topics related to her books and oracle cards. She's the author of *Assertiveness for Earth Angels*, *The Miracles of Archangel Michael*, and *Archangel Oracle Cards*, among many other works. She has appeared on *Oprah*, CNN, and *Good Morning America,* and has been featured in newspapers and magazines worldwide. For information on Doreen's work, please visit her at AngelTherapy.com or Facebook.com/Doreen Virtue444. To enroll in her online video courses, please visit www.EarthAngel.com.

ANGEL THERAPY®

Hay House Titles of Related Interest

YOU CAN HEAL YOUR LIFE, the movie,
starring Louise Hay & Friends
(available as a 1-DVD program and an expanded 2-DVD set)
Watch the trailer at: www.LouiseHayMovie.com

THE SHIFT, the movie, starring Dr. Wayne W. Dyer
(available as a 1-DVD program and an expanded 2-DVD set)
Watch the trailer at: www.DyerMovie.com

✳   ✳   ✳

*A COURSE IN MIRACLES MADE EASY: Mastering the Journey
from Fear to Love,* by Alan Cohen

*DESTRESSIFYING: The Real-World Guide to Personal Empower-
ment, Lasting Fulfillment, and Peace of Mind,* by davidji

*THE DIVINE NAME: Invoke the Sacred Sound That Can Heal
and Transform,* by Jonathan Goldman

LIFE LOVES YOU: 7 Spiritual Practices to Heal Your Life,
by Louise Hay and Robert Holden, Ph.D.

*RESILIENCE FROM THE HEART: The Power to Thrive
in Life's Extremes,* by Gregg Braden

*SHADOWS BEFORE DAWN: Finding the Light of Self-Love
Through Your Darkest Times,* by Teal Swan

*UPLIFTING PRAYERS TO LIGHT YOUR WAY: 200 Invocations
for Challenging Times,* by Sonia Choquette

All of the above are available at your local bookstore,
or may be ordered by contacting Hay House (see next page).

We hope you enjoyed this Hay House book. If you'd like to receive our online catalog featuring additional information on Hay House books and products, or if you'd like to find out more about the Hay Foundation, please contact:

Hay House, Inc., P.O. Box 5100, Carlsbad, CA 92018-5100
(760) 431-7695 or (800) 654-5126
(760) 431-6948 (fax) or (800) 650-5115 (fax)
www.hayhouse.com® • www.hayfoundation.org

Published and distributed in Australia by: Hay House Australia Pty. Ltd.,
18/36 Ralph St., Alexandria NSW 2015 • *Phone:* 612-9669-4299
Fax: 612-9669-4144 • www.hayhouse.com.au

Published and distributed in the United Kingdom by: Hay House UK, Ltd.,
Astley House, 33 Notting Hill Gate, London W11 3JQ
Phone: 44-20-3675-2450 • *Fax:* 44-20-3675-2451 • www.hayhouse.co.uk

Published and distributed in the Republic of South Africa by: Hay House SA
(Pty), Ltd., P.O. Box 990, Witkoppen 2068 • info@hayhouse.co.za
www.hayhouse.co.za

Published in India by: Hay House Publishers India, Muskaan Complex, Plot
No. 3, B-2, Vasant Kunj, New Delhi 110 070 • *Phone:* 91-11-4176-1620
Fax: 91-11-4176-1630 • www.hayhouse.co.in

Distributed in Canada by: Raincoast Books, 2440 Viking Way, Richmond,
B.C. V6V 1N2 • *Phone:* 1-800-663-5714 • *Fax:* 1-800-565-3770
www.raincoast.com

Take Your Soul on a Vacation

Visit www.HealYourLife.com® to regroup, recharge, and reconnect with your own magnificence. Featuring blogs, mind-body-spirit news, and life-changing wisdom from Louise Hay and friends.

Visit www.HealYourLife.com today!